THE INSTANT POT PRESSURE COOKER COOKBOOK

101 INCREDIBLE RECIPES FOR BUSY FAMILIES!

By

VIRGINIA HATHAWAY

Copyright © 2015

By Virginia Hathaway

TABLE OF CONTENTS

INTRODUCTION — 7

PRESSURE COOKING TIMES — 13

BREAKFASTS & YOGURT — 17

    APPLE CHERRY BREAKFAST RISOTTO — 18

    APPLESAUCE — 19

    BLUEBERRY CROISSANT PUDDING — 20

    BREAKFAST HASH — 21

    CINNAMON RAISIN BREAD PUDDING WITH CARAMEL PECAN SAUCE — 22

    BREAKFAST SANDWICHES — 24

    EGG MUFFINS — 25

    GOLDEN DUMPLINGS — 26

    HUEVOS RANCHEROS — 27

    OVERNIGHT OATMEAL — 28

    PERFECT HARD BOILED EGGS — 29

    PLAIN YOGURT — 30

    POTATO & BACON CASSEROLE — 31

    QUINOA FOR BREAKFAST — 32

    SAUSAGE & EGG BREAKFAST CASSEROLE — 33

    STEWED FRUIT — 34

    VEGAN YOGURT — 35

    WHEAT BERRY & VEGGIE BREAKFAST — 36

MAIN DISHES 37

BEEF AND BROCCOLI	38
BEEF PHO	40
BRISKET AND ONIONS	42
CHICKEN ALFREDO	43
CARNITAS	44
CHICKEN CHILI	46
CHICKEN MARSALA	48
CHICKEN AND DUMPLINGS	50
CHICKEN ALFREDO RICE CASSEROLE	51
CHINESE BEEF AND BOK CHOY	52
COQ AU VIN	54
CURRIED CHICKEN WITH CAULIFLOWER	56
CHICKEN MOLE	58
GARLIC CHICKEN WITH COUSCOUS	59
GARLIC HONEY TERIYAKI CHICKEN WINGS	60
GREEK TACOS	62
ITALIAN BRAISED PORK	64
LOADED SLOW-COOKER BAKED POTATOES	66
MUSHROOM CHICKEN CORDON BLEU	68
MEATLOAF	70
PESTO PENNE WITH ARTICHOKE HEARTS	71
RANCH PASTA SALAD	72
RED BEANS & RICE	74
SEAFOOD GUMBO	76

PORK CHOPS IN MUSHROOM GRAVY 78

SHRIMP PAELLA 79

SLOW-COOKER CORNED BEEF AND CABBAGE 80

SOY-CITRUS CHICKEN 82

STUFFED TURKEY BREAST ROLL 84

TERIYAKI CHICKEN 86

SMOKEY BEEF BRISKET 88

SIDE DISHES **89**

"BAKED" SWEET POTATOES 90

BUTTERNUT SQUASH RISOTTO 91

CHEESY POTATOES AU GRATIN 92

CANDIED YAMS 94

CORN & RICE SALAD 95

CRISPY POTATOES 96

CURRIED QUINOA 98

GARLIC VEGETABLES 100

GREEN BEANS & POTATOES 101

HOT POTATO SALAD 102

JEERA RICE 103

INDIAN RICE 104

MUSHROOM & PARSLEY POTATOES 106

RATATOUILLE 107

SEARED MARINATED ARTICHOKES 108

QUINOA SALAD 110

SEASONED ROOT VEGETABLES 112

STEAMED BROCCOLI 114

SWEET CARROTS 115

TAWA PULAO 116

VEGETABLE BIRYANI 118

VEGETABLE MEDLEY 120

SOUPS 121

BEAN AND BARLEY SOUP 122

CHICKEN TORTILLA SOUP 124

CREAM OF BROCCOLI 126

FRENCH ONION SOUP 128

FRESH LEMON & GARLIC LAMB STEW 129

GARLIC & CHICKEN STEW 130

HEARTY BEEF STEW 131

NEW ENGLAND CLAM CHOWDER 132

ONION CHICKEN SOUP 134

QUICK & EASY CHILI 135

PORK & HOMINY STEW 136

PUMPKIN SOUP WITH CHICKEN & ORZO 138

SEAFOOD CHOWDER 140

VEAL SHANK BARLEY SOUP 141

VIETNAMESE SEAFOOD STEW 142

VEAL STEW 144

DESSERTS 145

APPLE CINNAMON FLAN 146

APPLE CRUMB CAKE   148

CREAMY RICE PUDDING   149

BLUEBERRY PUDDING   150

CHOCOLATE CHIP CHEESECAKE   152

FUDGE   154

LEMON CRÈME   155

MEYER LEMON CHEESECAKE   156

PUMPKIN CHOCOLATE CHIP BUNDT CAKE   158

QUICK AND EASY HAZELNUT FLAN   160

STEAMED BREAD PUDDING   162

PEARS IN RED WINE   164

TAPIOCA PUDDING   165

INTRODUCTION

INSTANT POT

Congratulations if you've just purchased an Instant Pot pressure cooker! But be careful...you'll have to come up with some new activities to do with all the time you'll be saving and anyone who tries your food might think you've kidnapped a master chef and are holding them hostage. This thing truly is a "Magic Pot" and it will have you cooking like a famous chef. Seriously...with the push of a button, you'll know that whatever you desire will come out tasting amazing and be perfectly cooked. And because Instant Pot pressure cookers are so safe, they will completely change how you prepare food.

6-in-1

This incredible cooker is fast, simple and energy efficient. The convenient key pad contains the most common cooking features including sauté, steam, warm, rice, slow cook, pressure cook. This pot uses 70% less energy that convention methods and can cook the food up to five times faster. It's not the scary pressure cooker of the 1970's, but a new sleek model that is safe, reliable and easy to use. Cooking becomes a joy and meals are delicious, nutritious and quick.

7-in-1

This cooker is the newest model of the Instant Pot, and adds the unique and useful feature to make homemade yogurt. Just like the 6-in-1, this new model has 10 safety features including a locking lid, so the lid will not open if the contents are under pressure. In addition, like the 6-in-1, this pot has a delay cook timer for up to 24 hours. One of the brilliant features of this new design is an app that allows you to create new recipes. With this app and the pot's Bluetooth capabilities, cooking is made even easier.

COOKING METHODS

Braise

Braising is a type of cooking that uses moist heat to break down the tough connective tissue in meat. This allows the meat to become juicy and tender.

To Braise

1. Heat a small amount of oil on the sauté function and brown the meat on all sides.
2. Add the liquid and deglaze the pan, making sure to scrape any bits off the bottom.
3. Bring the liquid to a simmer.
4. Add an acidic ingredient – like tomatoes – to help break down the tissue.
5. Use the Meat/Stew function to cook at approximately 300°F to cook the meat for 1 – 5 hours.

Larger cuts of meat will take longer. Also remember that these tough cuts of meat are usually less expensive.

Sauté

Sautéing is a type of dry heat cooking. A very hot pan is used and a very little amount of fat. The food is cooked very quickly. Sautéing browns the surface of the food and adds delicious flavors and aromas. Most commonly, vegetables (especially onions and garlic) are sautéed to bring out their flavor.

Steam

Steaming is a moist heat type of cooking. Water is added to the pan and then the food is added in a rack or tray on top. The water heats and the steam then heats the food. Steaming is a great way to cook vegetables, allowing them to become tender but still keeping the color and nutrients that are so important.

Rice Cooker

The rice cooker function of the Instant Pot is wonderful. Rice cookers take away all the bother and worry of trying to remember to stir the rice, check on it and make sure it doesn't burn. Simply add the rice and water, shut the lid and turn it on. Come back 30 – 40 minutes later to delicious, tender and fluffy rice every time.

For white rice, use a 1:1 ratio. One cup of rice to one cup of water.
For brown rice or wild rice use a 1:1 ½ ratio. One cup of rice to one and half cups of water.

For brown and wild rice, try using vegetable or chicken broth instead of plain water. It adds more flavor to the rice.

Slow Cooker

Slow cooking is a great way to fix something in the morning, turn it on and have a meal ready at the end of the day. Slow cooking is wonderful for meats, soups and stews. Slow cooking on the low setting is about 200°F, while the high setting is about 300°F. The food rarely reaches more than boiling (212°F) temperature. This is a great way to cook meat that turns out tender and moist every time.

Pressure Cooker

Pressure cooking simply cooks the food in a sealed container. The seal keeps the steam from the cooking liquid trapped, allowing the pressure to rise. This cooks the food faster than traditional methods. The Instant Pot pressure cooker is simple and safe to use. With the built in safety features, the lid will not unlock if there is any pressure remaining in the container. This is a great way to cook meat, beans, desserts, breakfasts, soups, stews and just about anything else.

Yogurt (7-in-1)

The yogurt function in the 7-in-1 Instant Pot is a wonderful addition. Homemade yogurt is often healthier and less expensive than store bought yogurt. All that's needed is milk and a little yogurt or yogurt starter. If you like flavored yogurt, you can add the flavoring before cooking, or simply wait until afterwards and add a spoonful of your favorite jam for a little flavor and added sweet. Yogurt can be used as a great alternative to mayonnaise and sour cream in recipes.

1

PRESSURE COOKING TIMES

COMMON PRESSURE COOKING TIMES FOR VEGETABLES

Vegetable	Approximate Cooking Time (minutes)	Pressure Level
Artichoke, medium whole, without leaves	6 to 8	High
Artichoke, hearts	2 to 3	High
Asparagus, fine, whole	1 to 1 1/2	High
Beans, green, whole (fresh or frozen)	2 to 3	High
Beets, 1/4" (5 mm) slices	5 to 6	High

Broccoli, flowerets	2	High
Brussel sprouts, whole	4	High
Cabbage, red or green, 1/4" (5 mm) slices	1	High
Carrots, 1/4" (5 mm) slices	1	High
Carrots, 1" (25 mm) chunks	4	High
Cauliflower flowerets	2 to 3	High
Corn, kernels	1	High
Corn on the cob	3	High
Eggplant, 1/2" (10 mm) chunks	3	High
Endive, thickly cut	1 to 2	High
Green beans, whole (fresh or frozen)	2 to 3	High
Kale, coarsely chopped	2	High

Mixed vegetables, frozen	2 to 3	High
Okra, small pods	2 to 3	High
Onions, medium whole	2 to 3	High
Parsnips, 1" (25 mm) slices	2 to 4	High
Peas, green	1	High
Potatoes, cut into 1" (25 mm) cubes	5 to 7	High
Potatoes, new, whole small	5 to 7	High
Potatoes, whole large	10 to 12	High
Pumpkin, 2" (50 mm) slices	3 to 4	High
Red beet, small, whole	12	High
Rutabaga, 1" (25 mm) chunks	5	High
Spinach, fresh	1	Low

Spinach, frozen	4	High
Squash, acorn, halved	7	High
Squash, butternut, 1" (25 mm) slices	4	High
Sweet potato, 1 1/2" (40 mm) slices	5	High
Tomatoes, in quarters	2	High
Tomatoes, whole	3	High
Turnip, small, in quarters	3	High
Zucchini, 1/4" (5 mm) slices	2	High

2

BREAKFASTS & YOGURT

APPLE CHERRY BREAKFAST RISOTTO

SERVINGS: 4

This delicious and creamy breakfast is packed with nutrients. Using the pressure cooker makes this a quick and easy breakfast.

INGREDIENTS

2 Tbsp. butter
1 1/2 cups Arborio rice
2 large apples, cored and diced
1 1/2 tsp cinnamon
1/4 tsp salt
1/3 cup brown sugar
1 cup apple juice
3 cups milk (I used 1%)
1/2 cup dried cherries

PROCEDURE

1) Using the sauté mode, melt the butter in the Instant Pot. Add the rice and cook for 3 -4 minutes, stirring frequently.
2) Add the apples, spices and brown sugar.
3) Stir in the juice and milk.
4) Cook on high pressure for 6 minutes.
5) Use the quick release and remove the rice from the cooker. Gently stir in the cherries.
6) Serve hot, topped with more brown sugar, almonds and milk (if desired).

Nutrition Facts: Serving size: 1/4 of a recipe (15.2 ounces). Calories: 591.53, Total Fat: 9.84 g, Cholesterol: 29.91 mg, Sodium: 255.66 mg, Potassium: 422.97 mg, Total Carbohydrates: 114.65 g, Protein: 11.95 g

APPLESAUCE

SERVINGS: 12

This homemade applesauce is like no applesauce you've ever tasted. It goes really well on steel cut oatmeal in the morning, or by itself as a snack.

INGREDIENTS

3 lbs. apples, peeled, cored and quarter
¾ tsp ground cinnamon
1/3 cup unsweetened apple juice

PROCEDURE

1) Combine all the ingredients in the Instant Pot.
2) Cook on high pressure for 1 minute.
3) Allow the pressure to slowly release.
4) If desired, blend the applesauce in a blender or food processor, or use an immersion blender or food mill.
5) Serve warm or cold.

Nutrition Facts: Serving size: 1/12 of a recipe (4.2 ounces). Calories: 62.54, Total Fat: 0.2 g, Cholesterol: 0 mg, Sodium: 1.43 mg, Potassium: 129 mg, Total Carbohydrates: 16.57 g

BLUEBERRY CROISSANT PUDDING

SERVINGS: 10

This fresh twist on the traditional bread pudding is perfect for brunch.

INGREDIENTS

3 large croissants, cut up (about 5 to 5 1/2 cups)
1 cup fresh or frozen blueberries
1 package (8 oz.) cream cheese, softened
2/3 cup sugar
2 eggs
1 tsp vanilla
1 cup milk

PROCEDURE

1) In a heat safe bowl, place the croissants. Add the blueberries on top.
2) In a bowl, beat together the cream cheese, sugar, eggs and vanilla until well combined.
3) Add the milk to the cream cheese mixture and mix well.
4) Pour the egg mixture over the croissants, then allow the mixture to sit for 20 minutes.
5) Cook on high pressure for 20 minutes.
6) Allow the pressure to slowly release.
7) Serve warm topped with powdered sugar.

Nutrition Facts: Serving size: 1/10 of a recipe (3.6 ounces). Calories: 208.57, Total Fat: 10.74 g, Cholesterol: 69.4 mg, Sodium, 145.64 mg, Potassium: 106.7 mg, Total Carbohydrates: 24 g, Protein: 4.78 g

BREAKFAST HASH

SERVINGS: 4

This wholesome breakfast hash is simple to make yet hearty and filling. It will become a family favorite in no time.

INGREDIENTS

> *6 eggs, beaten*
> *1 cup grated cheese*
> *1/2 cup ham, sausage or bacon*
> *4 small potatoes, shredded*

PROCEDURE

1) Coat the pot with cooking spray and preheat.
2) Squeeze all the moisture out of the potatoes and brown the potatoes in the pot on sauté.
3) Meanwhile, beat the eggs.
4) Combine all the ingredients in the instant pot and add a 1/4 cup water.
5) Bring the pot to high pressure and then allow it to slow release.
6) Serve with a side of toast (if desired).

Nutrition Facts: Serving size: 1/4 of a recipe (10.1 ounces). Calories: 373.38, Total Fat: 15.4 g, Cholesterol: 310.63 mg, Sodium: 731.18 mg, Potassium: 905.75 mg, Total Carbohydrates: 31.25 g, Protein: 26.85 g

---

CINNAMON RAISIN BREAD PUDDING WITH CARAMEL PECAN SAUCE

SERVINGS: 8

This bread pudding is simply good for the soul. It is not too sweet, so it's perfect for breakfast.

INGREDIENTS

4 Tbsp. butter, melted
½ cup packed brown sugar
3 cups whole milk
3 eggs, beaten
1 tsp vanilla extract
1.2 tsp ground cinnamon
¼ tsp salt
7 thick slices cinnamon bread, cubed and toasted
½ cupraisins
Caramel Pecan Sauce (optional)
¾ cupbrown sugar
¼ cupcorn syrup
2 Tbsp. heavy cream
2 Tbsp. butter
½ tsp salt
1 tsp vanilla extract
½ cuppecans, toasted & chopped

PROCEDURE

1) Whisk together the butter, brown sugar, milk, eggs, vanilla, cinnamon & salt. Mix until well combined.
2) Add the bread and raisins. Allow the mixture to rest for 20 minutes before cooking so the bread can absorb the milk. Stir the mixture occasionally during the 20 minutes.
3) Pour the mixture into a glass or metal baking dish that will fit into the

cooker.

4) Cover the dish with foil, and use a long piece of foil to make a "handle" to lift the dish out with.

5) Add 1 ½ cups water to the cooker and place a trivet in the bottom.

6) Place the "handle" on top of the trivet and then place the bowl with the bread mixture on top.

7) Cook on high pressure for 20 minutes, then quickly release the pressure.

8) Remove and serve hot with the caramel sauce.

9) While the bread pudding is cooking, prepare the caramel sauce.

10) Combine the sugar, syrup, cream, butter and salt in a small saucepan and bring to a boil over medium heat, being sure to stir constantly.

11) Reduce heat once the mixture boils and continue to cook until the sugar completely dissolves.

12) Add the vanilla and nuts. Serve on top of the bread pudding.

Nutrition Facts: Serving size: 1/8 of a recipe (7.7 ounces). Calories: 146.61, Total Fat: 19.62 g, Cholesterol: 104.36 mg, Sodium: 460.47 mg, Potassium: 344.09 mg, Total Carbohydrates: 73.33 g, Protein: 9.96 g

BREAKFAST SANDWICHES

SERVINGS: 2

These sandwiches are delicious and quick. After trying them, you'll never go back to the drive thru!

INGREDIENTS

> 2 cups water
> Drop of olive oil
> 2 thin slices prosciutto, ham or meat of choice
> 2 eggs
> 2 Tbsp. cheddar cheese, grated
> 4 slices rye bread

PROCEDURE

1) Place a trivet in the bottom of the cooker. Add the water to the cooker.
2) Lightly grease the bottom of 2 ramekins.
3) Line the bottom of the ramekin with the slice of meat and then add the whole egg on top. The egg can be scrambled or whole.
4) Add fresh pepper and the cheese on top.
5) Cover the ramekins with foil and place in a steamer basket.
6) Place the basket on top of the trivet and cook on low pressure for 6 minutes.
7) Allow the pressure to slowly decrease.
8) While the pressure reduces, toast and butter (if desired) the bread.
9) Remove the ramekins from the Instant Pot and loosen the edge with a knife.
10) Tip the egg and meat mixture onto the slice of bread.
11) Serve immediately.

Nutrition Facts: Serving size: 1/2 of a recipe (13.7 ounces). Calories: 329.29, Total Fat: 12.85 g, Cholesterol: 210.26 mg, Sodium: 927.98 mg, Potassium: 275.98 mg,   Total Carbohydrates: 31.38 g, Protein: 20.88 g

---

EGG MUFFINS

SERVINGS: 4

INGREDIENTS

4 eggs
1/4 tsp lemon pepper seasoning
4 Tbsp. shredded cheddar/Jack cheese
1 green onion, diced
4 slices precooked bacon, crumbled

PROCEDURE

1) In the bottom of the cooker, place a trivet and add 1 1/2 cups of water.
2) In a large bowl, combine the eggs and lemon pepper. Beat well.
3) Lightly grease 4 small ramekins.
4) Evenly divide the cheese, bacon and green onion into the ramekins.
5) Pour the eggs into the ramekins and gently stir.
6) Place the ramekins on the trivet and cook on high pressure for 8 minutes.
7) Quickly release the pressure and serve immediately.

Nutrition Facts: Serving size: 1/4 of a recipe (2.5 ounces). Calories: 136.98, Total Fat: 9.42 g, Cholesterol: 200.08 mg, Potassium: 131.91 mg, Total Carbohydrates: 0.99 g, Protein: 11.32 g

---

GOLDEN DUMPLINGS

SERVINGS: 8

These wholesome dumplings work really well to make an elegant and special breakfast.

INGREDIENTS

> *2 cup(s) Self-rising Flour*
> *7 Tbsp. Butter, diced*
> *2 Eggs*
> *0.25 cup(s) Milk*
> *2 Lemons*
> *8 tablespoon(s) Golden Syrup*
> *2/3cup Brown Sugar*
> *4 Tbsp. Butter (extra)*
> *2 cup(s) Water*

PROCEDURE

1) Cut the butter into the flour until well combined.
2) Whisk together the eggs and milk.
3) Add the egg mixture to the flour, and add the lemon zest.
4) Make golf ball sized dumplings with the flour mixture.
5) In the bottom of the pressure cooker, combine the sugar, syrup and butter. Bring to a boil on the sauté mode.
6) Add the water and lemon juice, then gently drop in the dumplings.
7) Make sure the dumplings don't clump together.
8) Cook on low pressure for 5 minutes.
9) Allow the pressure to slowly release.
10) Serve immediately.

Nutrition Facts: Serving size: 1/8 of a recipe (6.2 ounces). Calories: 198.8, Total Fat: 11.95 g, Cholesterol: 73.21 mg, Sodium: 345.88 mg, Potassium: 173.93 mg, Total Carbohydrates: 21.73 g, Protein: 4.14 g

---

HUEVOS RANCHEROS

SERVINGS: 2

This traditional Mexican meal is a tasty breakfast and brings a unique flavor to your day. Cooking the egg with the water on low pressure gives it a light and fluffy texture.

INGREDIENTS

1/2 - 3/4 cup salsa
3 eggs
Tortillas or Tortilla Chips
Vegetable oil, butter or margarine (optional)
Salt and pepper to taste

PROCEDURE

1) Measure a ¼ cup of salsa into each of 2 ramekins.
2) Crack the eggs into a small container and whisk together.
3) Divide the eggs evenly between the ramekins.
4) Cover the ramekins with foil.
5) Place 1 cup of water in the Instant Pot and place a trivet or steamer in the water.
6) Place the ramekins on the trivet and cook on low pressure for 20 minutes.
7) Scoop the eggs out onto warm tortillas with a large spoon.
8) Serve immediately and garnish with additional salsa, guacamole, sour cream and cheese (if desired).

Nutrition Facts: Serving size: 1/2 of a recipe (6.3 ounces). Calories: 256.07, Total Fat: 13.22 g, Cholesterol: 283.97 mg, Sodium: 886.35 mg, Potassium: 348.03 mg, Total Carbohydrates: 21.1 g, Protein: 13.14 g

OVERNIGHT OATMEAL

SERVINGS: 4

Using the Instant Pot's slow cooker function, this oatmeal becomes both easy and heartwarming. Put this oatmeal on the night before and get up to a tasty and nutritious breakfast.

INGREDIENTS

> *1 cup steel cut oats*
> *1 cup dried cranberries*
> *1 cup dried figs*
> *4 cups water*
> *1/2 cup half-and-half*

PROCEDURE

1) Combine all ingredients in the slow cooker.
2) Cook, covered, on low for 8 – 9 hours. It can easily cook overnight.
3) Serve hot with additional fruit, brown sugar and cream, if desired.

Nutrition Facts: Serving size: 1/4 of a recipe (18.1 ounces). Calories: 791.14, Total Fat: 8.85 g, Cholesterol: 11.19 mg, Sodium: 19.46 mg, Potassium: 530.85 mg,   Total Carbohydrates: 172.53 g, Protein: 8.71 g

PERFECT HARD BOILED EGGS

SERVINGS: 4

These eggs are so easy to make in the Instant Pot. They come out perfectly every time and are so easy to peel.

INGREDIENTS

4 -6 eggs

PROCEDURE

1) Place a trivet in the bottom of the Instant Pot and add 1 cup of water.
2) Place the eggs on the trivet.
3) Cook on low for 6 minutes, then allow the pressure to slowly release.
4) Remove the eggs from the cooker and immerse in cold water.
5) Serve immediately or refrigerate immediately.

Nutrition Facts: Serving size: 1/4 of a recipe (1.8 ounces). Calories: 71.5, Total Fat, 4.76 g, Cholesterol: 186 mg, Sodium: 71 mg, Potassium: 69 mg,   Total Carbohydrates: 0.36 g, Protein: 6.28

PLAIN YOGURT

SERVINGS: 4

This old fashioned yogurt isn't sweetened or flavored - it's plain. It's perfect for dips and sauces as well as any recipe that calls for yogurt. Use yogurt as a replacement for sour cream in recipes. If you'd like to sweeten the yogurt to eat it as a snack, simply add a little honey and vanilla to the yogurt, or a spoonful of your favorite jam.

INGREDIENTS

1 qt milk (1% or 2%)
4 - 6 tsp yogurt or yogurt starter

PROCEDURE

1) Evenly divide the milk into clean pint jars.
2) Stir in the yogurt or starter, making sure there are no lumps.
3) Place the jars in the Instant Pot.
4) Turn on the yogurt setting.
5) Allow the yogurt to cook for 6 - 12 hours.
6) Refrigerate the yogurt for 24 hours before using.

Nutrition Facts: Serving size: 1/4 of a recipe (8.8 ounces). Calories: 122, Total Fat: 4.83 g, Cholesterol: 19.52 mg, Sodium: 114.68 mg, Potassium: 341.6 mg, Total Carbohydrates: 11.71 g, Protein: 9.05 g

POTATO & BACON CASSEROLE

SERVINGS: 6

This delicious casserole is another that is simple and easy to make. I love the aroma it gives my home on a weekend morning. The leftovers are great for a quick breakfast during the week.

INGREDIENTS

4 cups frozen hash browns
½ cuponion, diced
8oz. bacon, cooked and crumbled
1 cup cheddar cheese, shredded
6 oz. milk
6 large eggs
1 ½ tsp seasoned salt

PROCEDURE

1) Whisk the eggs in a bowl until well combined.
2) Add the milk and mix well.
3) Add the seasoned salt.
4) In a heat safe bowl, combine the hash browns, onion, bacon and cheese. Mix well.
5) Add the egg mixture and mix to combine.
6) Place a trivet on the bottom of the cooker and add 1 cup of water.
7) Place the bowl on top of the trivet and cook on high pressure for 15 minutes.
8) Allow the pressure to slowly release.
9) Brown in the oven, if desired.
10) Serve hot.

Nutrition Facts: Serving size: 1/6 of a recipe (10.2 ounces). Calories: 486.2, Total Fat: 28.23 g, Cholesterol: 249.62 mg Sodium: 1,687.16 mg, Potassium: 759.3 mg, Total Carbohydrates: 28.56 g, Protein: 28.94 g

---

QUINOA FOR BREAKFAST

SERVINGS: 4

This quinoa can be cooked just like rice. You'd never know it's not oatmeal. It is a marvelous way to start the day.

INGREDIENTS

> 2 cups brown rice
> 1 cup red quinoa
> 5 ½ cups water
> 1 tsp salt
> 1/3 cup coconut oil or butter
> ¼ cup agave (or sweetener of choice)
> Berries or fruit of choice, optional
> Cream, optional

PROCEDURE

1) Combine the rice, quinoa, water and salt in the cooker.
2) Cook on high pressure for 12 minutes.
3) Allow the pressure to release slowly.
4) Add the coconut oil and agave. Add more if needed.
5) Serve with fruit and cream, if desired.

Nutrition Facts: Serving size: 1/4 of a recipe (17 ounces). Calories: 630.92, Total Fat: 20.1 g, Cholesterol: 40.63 mg, Sodium: 605.52 mg, Potassium: 493.79 mg, Total Carbohydrates: 101.19 g, Protein: 11.89 g

---

SAUSAGE & EGG BREAKFAST CASSEROLE

SERVINGS: 8

This filling casserole has flavor and color. It's a happy family that begins the day with this.

INGREDIENTS

> 1 medium head broccoli, chopped
> 1 12-oz package sausage links, cooked and sliced
> 1 cup shredded Cheddar, divided
> 10 eggs
> 3/4 cup whipping cream
> 2 cloves garlic, minced
> 1/2 tsp salt
> 1/4 tsp pepper

PROCEDURE

1) Whisk together the eggs, cream, garlic, salt and pepper.
2) In a heat safe bowl, layer the half of the broccoli, sausage and cheese in the bowl. Repeat the layers until all the ingredients are used.
3) Gently pour the egg mixture over the broccoli and sausage mixture.
4) Cook on high pressure for 12 minutes.
5) Allow the pressure to slowly release.
6) Serve hot.

Nutrition Facts: Serving size: 1/8 of a recipe (5 ounces). Calories: 287.96, Total Fat: 22.47 g, Cholesterol: 290.6 mg, Sodium: 572.85 mg, Potassium: 203.64 mg, Total Carbohydrates: 2.44 g, Protein: 18.74 g

---

STEWED FRUIT

SERVINGS: 6

This is a great way to prepare dried fruits. It can be used for dessert or breakfast. The wine can be substituted for fruit juice as well. It's great paired with oatmeal or ice cream.

INGREDIENTS

1 cup red wine
1 cup water
¾ cuppacked brown sugar (or sweeten to taste)
1 cinnamon stick
2 lemon slices
1lb. mixed dried fruits

PROCEDURE

1) Combine the wine, water, sugar, cinnamon and lemon in the cooker.
2) Using the sauté function, bring the mixture to a boil and stir until the sugar has dissolved.
3) Add the fruit and stir to mix well.
4) Cook for 4 minutes on high pressure.
5) Serve hot.

Nutrition Facts: Serving size: 1/6 of a recipe (5.9 ounces). Calories: 350.72, Total Fat: 6.38 g, Cholesterol: 0 mg, Sodium: 4.97 mg, Potassium: 60.49 mg, Total Carbohydrates: 66.08 g, Protein: 0.46 g

---

VEGAN YOGURT

SERVINGS: 4

This yogurt is smooth and creamy - just like the traditional dairy ones. Using unsweetened soy milk provides a plain yogurt that is perfect for sauces, dips and cooking. Add a spoonful of jam and you'll have a deliciously flavored yogurt for a snack.

INGREDIENTS

1 qt unsweetened soy milk
4 teaspoons vegan yogurt or yogurt starter

PROCEDURE

1) Evenly divide the soy milk between 2 pint jars.
2) Mix in the yogurt starter or yogurt.
3) Place the jars in the instant pot and press the yogurt setting.
4) Remove the jars in 8 - 9 hours and refrigerate for at least 24 hours before using.

Nutrition Facts: Serving size: 1/4 of a recipe (8.8 ounces). Calories: 80.19, Total Fat: 4.01 g, Cholesterol: 0 mg, Sodium: 85.05 mg, Potassium: 298.89 mg,   Total Carbohydrates: 4.01 g, Protein: 7 g

---

WHEAT BERRY & VEGGIE BREAKFAST

SERVINGS: 6

The wheat berries provide a delicious nutty texture to this breakfast. This breakfast is colorful, tasty and packed with fiber and vitamins.

INGREDIENTS

2 cups white wheat berries
1 Tbsp. oil or butter
1 Tbsp. regular salt
2 medium potatoes sliced or cubed
2 cups sliced carrots
2 medium onions sliced
5 stalks celery sliced
2-4 cloves smashed garlic if desired
1 tsp poultry seasoning
1/8 tsp thyme

PROCEDURE

1) Soak the wheat berries in 2 quarts of water overnight.
2) The next morning, add enough water to make 6 ½ cups of water.
3) Place the wheat, water, potatoes and carrots in the Instant Pot on the multi-grain setting.
4) Meanwhile, lightly sauté the onions, celery and garlic in a little butter.
5) Once the wheat is cooked, add the sautéed vegetables.
6) Garnish with chopped flat leaf parsley and serve with a side of plain yogurt.

Nutrition: Serving size: 1/6 of a recipe (8.9 ounces). Calories: 325.76, Total Fat: 3.27 g, Cholesterol: 0.28 mg, Sodium: 1,243.98 mg, Potassium: 836.94 mg, Total Carbohydrates: 68.99 mg, Protein: 9.71 g

3

MAIN DISHES

BEEF AND BROCCOLI

SERVINGS: 6

Using the high pressure setting makes this traditional Asian meal a snap. The beef is tender and juicy with bright green broccoli that is packed with flavor and nutrients.

INGREDIENTS

1 1/2 lbs. boneless beef chuck roast, well-trimmed and sliced into thin strips
Dash of salt and pepper to taste
2 tsp olive oil
1 medium onion, finely chopped
4 cloves garlic, minced
1 cup beef broth
1/2 cup soy sauce
1/3 cup brown sugar
2 Tbsp. sesame oil
1/8 tsp red pepper flakes
1 lb. broccoli florets
3 Tbsp. water
3 Tbsp. cornstarch
Toasted sesame seeds for garnish, optional

PROCEDURE

1) Season the roast with salt and pepper on all sides.
2) Brown the meat in the Instant Pot on sauté mode. Do not crowd the meat, work in batches.
3) Once the meat is cooked, add the onion and garlic to the pot. Cook for 2 – 3 minutes, or until the onion begins to soften.
4) Add the broth, soy sauce, brown sugar, sesame oil, and red pepper flakes to the pot. Stir until the sugar dissolves and the mixture is thoroughly combined.
5) Add the beef.

6) Cook on high pressure for 12 minutes
7) Meanwhile, lightly steam in broccoli in the microwave or on the stove until it is tender.
8) Once the beef is done, use the quick pressure release.
9) Combine the cornstarch and water. Stir until the mixture is smooth and no lumps remain.
10) Add the cornstarch to the sauce in the Instant Pot, while on sauté mode.
11) Bring the sauce to a boil and stir until it thickens.
12) Add the broccoli
13) Serve hot on a bed of rice and garnish with sesame seeds (if using).

Nutrition Facts: Serving size: 1/6 of a recipe (10.6 ounces). Calories: 497.79, Total Fat: 34.19 g, Cholesterol: 79.38 mg, Sodium: 946.14 mg, Potassium: 676.07 mg, Total Carbohydrates: 23.92 g, Protein: 24.31 g

BEEF PHO

SERVINGS: 8

This traditional Vietnamese beef stew is full of flavor, texture and nutrients. You'll love how easy it is to make, but you'll really love the incredible flavor.

INGREDIENTS

2 medium yellow onions, slice in half (skin on)

4-inch piece of ginger, sliced in half

5lbs. beef soup bones (leg and knuckle bones recommended)

5 whole star anise

6 whole cloves

1 cinnamon stick, 3 inches

1 Tbsp. coriander seeds

1 Tbsp. fennel seeds

1 black cardamom pod

1lb. beef chuck, rump, brisket, cross rib roast (2×4-inch pieces)

1 1/2 Tbsp. salt

4 Tbsp. fish sauce

1 oz. rock sugar or regular granulated sugar

1 1/2 -2 lbs. banh pho fresh or dried rice noodles, cooked according to package directions

3-4 green onions, sliced (green part only)

Black pepper, ground

1/3 cup cilantro, chopped

2 cups fresh mint

3 cups fresh basil (Thai basil, if you can get it)

2 cups mung bean sprouts

Thai chilies, sliced

1-2 limes, cut into wedges

Sriracha sauce

Hoisin sauce

PROCEDURE

1) Broil the onions and ginger for 10 – 15 minutes. Be sure to turn over halfway through. Set aside.
2) Place the beef bones a large pot and cover with cold water. Bring the bones to a boil and cook for 2 minutes.
3) Drain the bones. Place the bones in the Instant Pot and add 3 – 4 quarts of water.
4) Add the anise, cloves, cinnamon, coriander, fennel, cardamom beef, slat, fish sauce and sugar.
5) Cook on high pressure for 1 hour.
6) Strain the broth through a mesh sieve. Reserve the beef broth for other recipes. It will store in the refrigerator for up to 1 week.
7) Thinly slice the beef across the grain. Serve the beef over a bed of noodles with thinly sliced onions.
8) Ladle sauce over the noodles and garnish with cilantro, mint, basil, bean sprouts, chilies, lime wedges and sauce (if desired).

Nutrition Facts: Serving size: 1/8 of a recipe (9.5 ounces). Calories: 296.86, Total Fat: 11.18 g, Cholesterol: 48.2 mg, Sodium: 2,143.27 mg, Potassium: 438.96 mg, Total Carbohydrates: 35.54 g, Protein: 14.9 g

BRISKET AND ONIONS

SERVINGS: 6

The brisket comes from the lower chest portion of the cow. This cut can be tough, but cooking it on the slow cooker setting for 6 hours allows this meat to become tender and delicious. The onions add a wonderful flavor to the beef.

INGREDIENTS

> 1 large yellow onion, thinly sliced
> 2 garlic cloves, smashed and peeled
> 1 first cut of beef brisket (4 pounds), trimmed of excess fat
>   Coarse salt and ground pepper
> 2 cups low-sodium chicken broth
> 2 Tbsp. chopped fresh parsley leaves, for serving

PROCEDURE

1) Combine the onion and garlic in the Instant Pot.
2) Liberally season the brisket with salt and pepper. Add to the cooker. Be sure to place the fat side up in the cooker.
3) Add the 2 cups of broth and then cook on the slow cooker setting, covered, on high for 6 hours.
4) Remove the brisket from the pot and slice thinly across the grain.
5) Serve garnished with onions and parsley.

Nutrition Facts: Serving size: 1/6 of a recipe (14.8 ounces). Calories: 785.54, Total Fat: 58.14 g, Cholesterol: 205.63 mg, Sodium: 484.81 mg, Potassium: 975.52 mg, Total Carbohydrates: 3.45 g, Protein: 57.8 g

CHICKEN ALFREDO

SERVINGS: 3

The Instant Pot makes this chicken Alfredo quick and easy. The chicken is moist and tender. The creamy Alfredo provides a perfect sauce for this pasta dish. Serve with green beans, peas or carrots to add color to the meal.

INGREDIENTS

8 oz. (225 grams) dried pasta, egg noodles or fettuccine
1 15 ounce (425 grams) jar of Alfredo sauce
1 cup diced, cooked chicken
2 tsp chicken base
1 Tbsp. roasted garlic
½ tsp coarsely ground pepper
Parmesan cheese for garnish (optional)

PROCEDURE

1) In the Instant Pot, combine the pasta, chicken, chicken base, and 2 cups cold water.
2) Cook on high pressure for 2 minutes. Then turn the Instant Pot to the "Keep Warm" function.
3) One pressure has released, drain any excess water from the cooker.
4) Add the garlic to the Alfredo sauce and gently stir the sauce into the chicken and pasta mixture in the Instant Pot.
5) Add the pepper and mix well.
6) Serve hot, garnish with parmesan cheese, if desired.

Nutrition Facts: Serving size: 1/3 of a recipe (10.3 ounces). Calories: 719.22, Total Fat: 35.43 g, Cholesterol: 199.47 mg, Sodium: 1,338.98 mg, Potassium: 339.53 mg, Total Carbohydrates: 63.67 g. Protein: 36.85 g

---

CARNITAS

SERVINGS: 8

Carnitas are a traditional Mexican meal where the meat is braised in oil. The pressure cooker makes this meal quick and easy with the meat ending up tender and juicy. You'll love the combination of flavors.

INGREDIENTS

2 Tbsp. olive oil
2 tsp kosher salt
1 tsp ground cumin
1/2 tsp ancho or chipotle chili powder
1/2 tsp black pepper
3 lbs. boneless pork shoulder roast, cut into 2-inch chunks
1 onion, sliced
3 cloves garlic, smashed with the flat part of a knife
2 tsp dried oregano
1 cinnamon stick (3 inch)
1 1/2 cups strained fresh orange juice
1/2 cup strained fresh lime juice

PROCEDURE

1) In a small bowl, combine the oil, salt, cumin, pepper and chili powder. Mix well.
2) Mix together the pork and spice mixture.
3) Brown the pork in the Instant Pot on sauté.
4) Add the onion, garlic, oregano, cinnamon, orange and lime juice.
5) Mix well.
6) Cook on high pressure for 25 minutes.
7) Preheat the broiler.
8) Remove the contents of the pot and drain off the fat. Shred the pork.
9) Place the pork on a baking sheet and pour 1 cup of the liquid over the meat.
10) Broil for 5 – 8 minutes, or until the pork begins to turn crisp.

11) Stir the pork and broil for another 3 – 5 minutes.
12) Serve the pork on tortillas and topped with avocado, salsa and cheese.

Nutrition Facts: Serving size: 1/8 of a recipe (9 ounces). Calories: 382.3, Total Fat: 24.63 g, Cholesterol: 105.4 mg, Sodium: 578.76 mg, Potassium: 694.32 mg,   Total Carbohydrates: 8.71 g, Protein: 30.39 g

CHICKEN CHILI

SERVINGS: 6

This chicken chili is a delicious change from the traditional beef or vegetarian chili. Using the slow cooker makes this simple and easy to prepare - just put it in the pot in the morning and you've got a dinner ready to go in the evening!

INGREDIENTS

2 lbs. ground chicken, coarsely ground preferred
3 Tbsp. chili powder, plus 2 teaspoons
1 (15-ounce) can kidney beans, drained and rinsed
1 (15-ounce) can white beans, drained and rinsed
2 (28-ounce) cans diced fire roasted tomatoes
1 medium sweet potato (about 10 ounces), peeled and shredded
1 (15-ounce) can low-sodium chicken broth
1/4 cup instant tapioca (recommended: Minute tapioca)
1 to 2chipotle chilies in adobo sauce with seeds, chopped
2 Tbsp. soy sauce
1 Tbsp. kosher salt
1 Tbsp. onion powder
2 tsp granulated garlic
1 tsp dried oregano
1 tsp ground cumin
1/4 tsp ground cinnamon
Pinch ground cloves
1/2 to 3/4 cup lager-style beer, optional
Toppings: Sour cream, shredded Cheddar or Jack cheese, chopped scallions, and chopped pickled jalapenos

PROCEDURE

1) Reserve 2 teaspoons of chili powder and the beer (if using). Add all the rest of the ingredients into the Instant Pot.
2) Stir together and cook on the low slow cooker setting for 6 - 8 hours.

3) Just before serving add the reserved chili powder and beer (if using).
4) Season to taste with salt and pepper.
5) Serve hot with the toppings of choice.

Nutrition Facts: Serving size: 1/6 of a recipe (22.7 ounces). Calories: 920.32, Total Fat: 16.5 g, Cholesterol: 142.16 mg, Sodium: 1,706.51 mg, Potassium: 3,237.61 mg, Total Carbohydrates: 112.66 g, Protein:84.27 g

CHICKEN MARSALA

SERVINGS: 6

This delicious Italian dish features herbed chicken that is served with a sweet Marsala and mushroom sauce. The pressure cooker makes this simple and quick.

INGREDIENTS

4 slices peppered bacon, diced
3 lbs. boneless, skinless chicken thighs, well-trimmed
Salt and pepper
1/2 cup sweet Marsala wine
1 cup chicken broth
1 Tbsp. vegetable oil
3 Tbsp. butter, divided
Chopped parsley or chives for garnish
8 oz. mushrooms, sliced
2 Tbsp. cornstarch
3 Tbsp. cold water
2 Tbsp. chopped parsley

PROCEDURE

1) Using the browning function, brown the bacon until crisp. Be sure to stir frequently so it doesn't burn.
2) Remove the bacon and drain on paper towels.
3) Season the chicken with salt and pepper. Brown the chicken in the bacon fat until it's evenly browned.
4) Add the wine to the pot. Deglaze the pot, being sure to scrap all the bits off the bottom.
5) Return the chicken to the pot.
6) Cook on high pressure for 10 minutes. Be sure to start the timer for 10 minutes once it has reached pressure.
7) Meanwhile, whisk together the cornstarch and water.

8) Once the chicken has finished cooking, add the cornstarch mixture to the pot and stir until it's dissolved and has reached the desired consistency.
9) Bring the mixture to a boil.
10) Add the mushrooms. Stir to mix well.
11) Season to taste.
12) Serve with the crumbled bacon on top. Garnish with parsley, if desired.

Nutrition Facts: Serving size: 1/6 of a recipe (5.9 ounces). Calories: 254.92, Total Fat: 20.67 g, Cholesterol: 49.51 mg, Sodium: 357.1 mg, Potassium: 288.5 mg, Total Carbohydrates: 4.75 g, Protein: 9.41 g

CHICKEN AND DUMPLINGS

SERVINGS: 8

This delicious and traditional chicken and dumplings recipe is the ultimate comfort food. It's simple and easy to prepare with the slow cooker setting.

INGREDIENTS

4 boneless, skinless chicken breast halves
¼ tsp poultry seasoning
¼ tsp paprika
¼ tsp pepper
2 cans (10.5 oz. each) condensed cream of chicken soup, undiluted
1 can (14.5 oz.) chicken broth
1 1/2 cups water
2 tubes (10 oz. each) refrigerated biscuit dough, torn into pieces
Chopped parsley, for serving (optional)

PROCEDURE

1) Season the chicken with the pepper, paprika and poultry seasoning. Place the chicken in the Instant Pot.
2) In a good medium sized bowl, whisk the soup, broth and water. Gently pour this mixture over your chicken.
3) Cook on the Instant Pot's slow cooker setting, covered, for 5 – 6 hours at the high setting.
4) Take out the chicken and chop into small pieces. Put the chicken back in the pot.
5) Add the biscuit dough and mix to be sure that the dough is thoroughly submerged.
6) Cook for an additional 90 minutes on high, or up to when the dough has been completely cooked.
7) Serve garnished with a dash of chopped parsley.

Nutrition Facts: Serving size: 1/8 of a recipe (12.8 ounces). Calories: 394.24, Total Fat: 10.96 g, Cholesterol: 82.62 mg , Sodium: 1,533.58 mg, Potassium: 635.75 mg,   Total Carbohydrates: 39.52 g, Protein: 32.7 g

---

CHICKEN ALFREDO RICE CASSEROLE

SERVINGS: 6

This casserole is a delicious change from the traditional chicken Alfredo with pasta. The slow cooker setting of the Instant Pot makes this meal nearly effortless to prepare.

INGREDIENTS

4 cloves of garlic, minced
1 ½ cups rice or brown rice
2 breasts of chicken, sliced
2 Tbsp. of butter
2 oz. of cream cheese
½ tsp of salt
¼ tsp pepper
2 Tbsp. parmesan cheese plus more for garnish
2 ½ cups half and half cream
½ cupchicken broth
1 head of broccoli, chopped

PROCEDURE

1) Sauté the garlic in the Instant Pot.
2) Add the rice, chicken, butter, cream cheese, salt, pepper, parmesan cream and broth. Mix well.
3) Cook on high on the slow cooker setting for 2 – 3 hours.
4) Add the broccoli and stir to combine. Cook for an additional 20 minutes.
5) Serve topped with fresh parmesan.

Nutrition Facts: Serving size: 1/6 of a recipe (12.7 ounces). Calories: 467.98, Total Fat: 22.29 g, Cholesterol: 83.71 mg, Sodium: 412.58 mg, Potassium: 708.65 mg, Total Carbohydrates: 53.02 g, Protein: 20.89

CHINESE BEEF AND BOK CHOY

SERVINGS: 4

Bok Choy provides a simple and delicate flavor that blends beautifully with the ginger, leeks and sauce. The beef is tender and flavorful.

INGREDIENTS

4 leeks (white and light green parts only), trimmed, halved lengthwise and cut into 1-inch pieces
6 cloves garlic, unpeeled
4 thin slices ginger, unpeeled
1 red jalapeno pepper, seeded and thinly sliced
3 Tbsp. all-purpose flour
1 1/2 lbs. beef chuck roast, trimmed
1/4 cup hoisin sauce
1/4 cup Shaoxing rice wine, mirin or dry sherry
3 Tbsp. soy sauce
2 Tbsp. packed light brown sugar
4 heads baby bok choy, cut crosswise into 2-inch pieces
2 cups cooked white rice, for serving

PROCEDURE

1) In the Instant Pot, combine the leeks, garlic, ginger and jalapeno. Add the flour and toss to completely coat the vegetables.
2) Add the beef to the vegetable mixture.
3) In a small bowl, whisk together the hoisin sauce, rice wine, soy sauce, brown sugar and 1/3 cup warm water.
4) Add the sauce mixture to the Instant Pot. Cook on low, covered, for 7 hours.
5) Remove the meat from the pot and thinly slice across the grain. Place the beef back into the pot and add the bok choy.
6) Cook on high for about 5 minutes, or until the bok choy begins to wilt.

7) Serve over a bed of rice.

Nutrition Facts: Serving size: 1/4 of a recipe (41.3 ounces). Calories: 817.42, Total Fat: 43.69 g, Cholesterol: 119.55 mg, Sodium: 1,308.85 mg, Potassium: 2,877.38 mg, Total Carbohydrates: 68.39 g, Protein: 47.32 g

COQ AU VIN

SERVINGS: 6

This traditional French dish has a succulent chicken braised in wine with garlic and mushrooms.

INGREDIENTS

1/2 cup diced bacon
3 lbs. boneless, skinless chicken thighs, well-trimmed
Salt and pepper
1 medium yellow onion, chopped
2 cloves garlic, chopped
1 cup red wine
1 cup chicken broth
1 Tbsp. tomato paste
1 bay leaf
2 sprigs thyme
2 carrots, sliced
1 Tbsp. vegetable oil
1 Tbsp. butter
1 package (12 ounces) white mushrooms, quartered
2 Tbsp. cornstarch
3 Tbsp. cold water
2 Tbsp. chopped parsley

PROCEDURE

1) Cook the bacon on sauté mode until crisp. Be sure to stir frequently so that it doesn't burn.
2) Remove the bacon, leaving the fat.
3) Brown the chicken in the leftover bacon fat.
4) Add the onions and garlic, cook for 3 – 5 minutes or until the onions are softened.
5) Add the wine and stir to make sure all the bits are off the bottom of the pan. Cook until most of the wine has cooked off.

6) Add the broth, tomato paste, bay leaf, thyme and carrots.
7) Cook on high pressure for 10 minutes.
8) Meanwhile, sauté the mushrooms in the oil and butter in a large pan until they are golden brown. Season the mushrooms with salt and pepper.
9) Mix together the cornstarch and water until no lumps remain.
10) Add the cornstarch to the Instant Pot and bring the mixture to a boil.
11) Once the mixture reaches its desired consistency, add the mushrooms and stir.
12) Season to taste with salt and pepper.
13) Serve topped with bacon and parsley.

Nutrition Facts: Serving size: 1/6 of a recipe (7.1 ounces). Calories: 208.43, Total Fat: 11.35, Cholesterol: 31.56 mg, Sodium: 409.62 mg, Potassium: 314.01 mg, Total Carbohydrates: 11.81 g, Protein: 7.73 g

---

CURRIED CHICKEN WITH CAULIFLOWER

SERVINGS: 4

This curried chicken is moist and flavorful, but not too spicy. The preparation is simple and easy.

INGREDIENTS

3 Tbsp. canola oil
6 cloves garlic, minced
2 inch piece fresh ginger, minced
1/3 to 1/2 cup prepared South Asian curry paste (recommended: Patak)
3 cups chicken broth, low-sodium canned, or homemade
2 cups whole milk plain yogurt
6 bone-in skinless chicken thighs, about 2 1/4 pounds
1 1/2 Tbsp. kosher salt
Freshly ground black pepper
1 (1 pound) bag red lentils, picked over (2 1/4 cups)
1 head cauliflower, broken into large florets
2 (16-ounce) cans chickpeas, drained and rinsed
1 bunch fresh mint or cilantro leaves, chopped
1 lemon, cut in wedges

PROCEDURE

1) Sauté the garlic and ginger in a large skillet with the oil. Cook, stirring frequently, until fragrant.
2) Add the curry paste and cook for an additional 2 minutes.
3) Whisk in the broth and cook for 1 more minute.
4) Pour the broth combination into the Instant Pot.
5) Whisk in the yogurt.
6) Season each piece of chicken with salt and pepper.
7) Add the chicken and lentils to the Instant Pot.
8) Cook on high in the slow cooker setting for 3 hours.

9) Add the cauliflower and chickpeas. Cook on high for an additional 3 hours.
10) Serve hot, garnished with the mint or cilantro and a wedge of lemon.

Nutrition Facts: Serving size: 1/4 of a recipe (35.2 ounces). Calories: 1,062.98, Total Fat: 20.9 g, Cholesterol: 88.36 mg, Sodium: 3,601.26 mg, Potassium: 2,926.33 mg, Total Carbohydrates" 145.55 g, Protein: 76.51 g

CHICKEN MOLE

SERVINGS: 6

The unique chocolate adobo sauce makes this traditional chicken mole a delicious go-to meal.

INGREDIENTS

4 lbs. boneless, skinless chicken thighs (about 12)
Coarse salt
1 can (28 ounces) whole tomatoes
1 medium yellow onion, roughly chopped
2 dried ancho chilies, stemmed
1 large chipotle chili in adobo sauce
1/2 cup sliced almonds, toasted
1/4 cup raisins
3 oz. bittersweet chocolate, finely chopped (1/2 cup)
3 garlic cloves, smashed and peeled
3 Tbsp. extra-virgin olive oil
3/4 tsp ground cumin
1/2 tsp ground cinnamon
Fresh cilantro leaves, for serving

PROCEDURE

1) Liberally season the chicken with salt and pepper. Add to the Instant Pot.
2) Puree the remaining ingredients (except the cilantro) in a blender or food processor until they are smooth.
3) Add the mixture to the chicken and cook on the slow cooker setting, covered, on high for 4 hours or low for 8 hours.
4) Serve the chicken garnished with cilantro.

Nutrition Facts: Serving size: 1/6 of a recipe (8.6 ounces). Calories: 294.91, Total Fat: 21.52 g, Cholesterol: 22.69 mg, Sodium: 269.73 mg, Potassium: 679.44 mg, Total Carbohydrates: 22.06 g, Protein: 11.65 g

GARLIC CHICKEN WITH COUSCOUS

SERVINGS: 4

This succulent garlic chicken has delicious flavor. The slow cooker setting produces chicken that is moist and tender.

INGREDIENTS

1 whole chicken (3 1/2 to 4 pounds), cut into 6 to 8 pieces and patted dry
Coarse salt and ground pepper
1 Tbsp. extra-virgin olive oil
1 medium yellow onion, halved and thinly sliced
6 garlic cloves, halved
2 tsp dried thyme
1 cup dry white wine, such as Sauvignon Blanc
1/3 cup all-purpose flour
1 cup couscous
Chopped fresh parsley, for serving

PROCEDURE

1) Liberally season the chicken with salt and pepper. Sauté the chicken in the Instant Pot until it is an even golden brown.
2) Add the onion, garlic and thyme to the cooker.
3) In a small bowl, whisk together the wine and flour. Gently add it to the cooker.
4) Cook on the slow cooker setting, covered for 3 – 4 hours on high or 6 – 7 hours on low.
5) Before serving, cook couscous according to the package directions.
6) Serve the couscous topped with the chicken and sauce. Garnish with the parsley.

Nutrition Facts: Serving size: 1/4 of a recipe (12 ounces). Calories: 432.72, Total Fat: 11.84 g, Cholesterol: 145.15 mg, Sodium: 271.21 mg, Potassium: 925.78 mg, Total Carbohydrates: 21.56 g, Protein: 51.42 g

---

GARLIC HONEY TERIYAKI CHICKEN WINGS

SERVINGS: 6

These delicious wings have an amazing sauce they are cooked in. The sauce is thick and has hints of garlic, honey and ginger. These are perfect for a get together or large gathering, but also work wonderfully for a family meal.

INGREDIENTS

2 lbs. chicken wings

TERIYAKI SAUCE:

½ cup water
2 Tbsp. gluten free soy sauce (or regular if not gluten sensitive)
3 Tbsp. honey
2 garlic cloves, finely minced
½ tsp garlic powder
¼ tsp ground ginger
1 Tbsp. cornstarch
1 Tbsp. cold water
Sesame seeds, for garnish

PROCEDURE

FOR THE TERIYAKI SAUCE:

1) Combine the soy sauce, water, giner and garlic powder in a saucepan on medium heat. Simmer for 10 minutes.
2) Meanwhile, stir the cornstarch in with water. Once the sauce has simmered for 10 minutes, whisk in the cornstarch mix.
3) Turn off the heat and set aside.
4) Combine the wings to the sauce in the Instant Pot. Cook on slow cooker at high for approximately 3 to 4 hours or low for 6 – 8 hours.

5) Serve garnished with some sesame seeds.

Nutrition Facts: Serving size: 1/6 of a recipe (1.7 ounces). Calories: 71.16, Total Fat: 2.16 g, Cholesterol: 5.13 mg, Sodium: 184.34 mg, Potassium: 40.99 mg, Total Carbohydrates: 11.36 g, Protein: 2.34 g

GREEK TACOS

SERVINGS: 8

These tacos have a wonderful and moist pork topped with a flavorful tzatziki sauce. Using the pressure cooker makes this a quick fix, but the pork stays tender and moist.

INGREDIENTS

4 lbs. boneless picnic pork shoulder, trimmed and cut into 1-inch cubes
1/2 tsp salt
1/4 tsp pepper
1 tsp marjoram
2 Tbsp. olive oil
1/2 cup fresh squeezed lemon juice
1/4 cup water

TZATZIKI SAUCE:

1 small cucumber, peeled, seeded and shredded
1/4 tsp salt
1 cup plain Greek yogurt
1 Tbsp. lemon juice
1 tsp dried dill weed
1 clove garlic, minced or pressed
1/8 tsp pepper

PROCEDURE

1) In a small bowl, combine the marjoram, salt, pepper and olive oil. Rub the mixture over the pork shoulder.
2) In the Instant Pot, combine the lemon juice along with the water. Add the pork to the liquid.
3) Cook on high pressure for 25 minutes.
4) Remove the pork from the liquid with tongs or slotted spoon.

5) Serve the pork on pita bread with tomatoes (diced), tzatziki sauce and lettuce.

TZATZIKI SAUCE:

1) Combine the cucumber and salt in a fine strainer. Let the cucumber drain for 10 – 15 minutes.
2) Rinse the cucumber to remove any remaining salt.
3) Take a mid-sized bowl and combine the cucumber, lemon juice, yogurt, dill, pepper and garlic. Mix well to combine. Keep refrigerated.

Nutrition Facts: Serving size: 1/8 of a recipe (11.8 ounces). Calories: 674.63, Total Fat: 51.92 g, Cholesterol: 131.54 mg, Sodium: 2,650.95 mg, Total Carbohydrates: 2.32 g, Protein: 46.69 g

ITALIAN BRAISED PORK

SERVINGS: 4

Braising pork leads to an incredibly tender and moist meat. This goes perfectly over couscous, polenta, rice or pasta.

INGREDIENTS

2 Tbsp. olive oil
2 1/2 lbs. boneless pork shoulder
Coarse salt and pepper
1 large yellow onion, diced small
3 cloves garlic, minced
1 stalk celery, diced small
3/4 tsp fennel seeds
1/2 cup dry red wine, such as Cabernet Sauvignon or Merlot
1 can (28 ounces) crushed tomatoes
4 cups prepared couscous, for serving

PROCEDURE

1) Season the pork with salt and pepper. Brown the seasoned pork in a large skillet over medium high heat. Make sure to brown the pork evenly on all sides.
2) Remove the pork from the skillet and place it in the Instant Pot.
3) Add the onion, garlic, celery and fennel to the same skillet the pork was cooked in.
4) Sauté until the onion is translucent, about 3 - 4 minutes.
5) Add the wine to the pan and continue to cook until the wine is reduced by half. Make sure to scrape all of the browned scraps off the bottom of the pan.
6) Add the wine mixture to the pork. Add the tomatoes to the pork.
7) Cook on the slow cooker setting on high, covered, for 4 hours, or low for 8 hours. The pork should be tender.

8) Place the pork on a cutting board and shred the meat into small pieces. Make sure to discard any pieces of fat while shredding the meat.
9) Separate the fat from the sauce and discard the fat.
10) Serve the pork over the couscous and top with the sauce.

Nutrition Facts: Serving size: 1/4 of a recipe (23 ounces). Calories: 830.59, Total Fat: 42.34 g, Cholesterol: 175.77 mg, Sodium: 398.63 mg, Potassium: 1,362.86 mg, Total Carbohydrates: 47.01 g, Protein: 57.03 g

LOADED SLOW-COOKER BAKED POTATOES

SERVINGS: 4

These delicious potatoes are packed with flavor and color. Using the slow cooker is a great way to make this a convenient meal for a busy night - prepare in the morning and you've got a tasty meal ready when you come home.

INGREDIENTS

4 medium russet potatoes
2 Tbsp. olive oil
10 oz. cremini mushrooms, trimmed and quartered
1 bunch broccoli, cut into small florets, stalks peeled and cut into 1/2-inch pieces
Salt and pepper
1/4 to 1/2 cup vegetable or chicken broth, hot
2/3 cup low-fat plain yogurt, room temperature

PROCEDURE

1) Wash the potatoes and pierce the skin with a fork or knife. Wrap each potato and place it in the cooking container of the Instant Pot.
2) Cook on the slow cooker setting, covered, until tender, about 8 hours on low.
3) About 10 minutes before serving, cook the mushrooms in a large skillet on medium high heat with the oil.
4) Cook for 2 minutes and then add the broccoli. Cook for 5 - 8 minutes, stirring frequently, until the broccoli is crisp-tender.
5) Cut open the potatoes and remove the meat from the skins. Place the potato flesh in a medium bowl and add the broth and yogurt.
6) Mix well and season with salt and pepper. Divide the mixture back into the potato skins.

7) Top each potato with the mushroom and broccoli mixture. Serve hot.

Nutrition Facts: Serving size: 1/4 of a recipe (19.1 ounces). Calories: 423.24, Total Fat: 8.47g, Cholesterol: 2.45, Sodium: 148.78 mg, Potassium: 2,324.53 mg,   Total Carbohydrates: 74.93 g, Protein: 15.67 g

MUSHROOM CHICKEN CORDON BLEU

SERVINGS: 4

This chef-worthy dish is delicious. The combination of the ham, mushrooms and Swiss are a rich and tasty combination.

INGREDIENTS

4 skinless, boneless chicken breasts, pounded out flat
4 slices black forest ham
4 slices Swiss cheese
Salt and pepper
1 Tbsp. butter
1 Tbsp. canola oil
½ tsp each dried thyme and tarragon
¼ tsp pepper and 1 tsp. salt
1-10 oz. cream of mushroom soup
½ cuphalf and half cream
½ cupsliced mushrooms
Toothpicks
Mashed potatoes

PROCEDURE

1) Place the chicken on a flat surface and top each breast with one slice of ham and then one slice of Swiss cheese.
2) Roll the chicken and secure with toothpicks or string.
3) Season the chicken with salt and pepper.
4) Brown the chicken in the Instant Pot.
5) Meanwhile, in a medium bowl, combine the soup, cream, thyme, tarragon, salt and pepper.
6) Once the chicken is browned, gently pour the soup mixture over the top.
7) Cook on low for 4 – 5 hours.
8) Slice the chicken into ¾-inch slices before serving.

9) Serve hot with a side of mashed potatoes topped with the mushroom gravy.

Nutrition Facts: Serving size: 1/4 of a recipe (16.7 ounces). Calories: 644.12, Total Fat: 32.37 g, Cholesterol: 212.27 mg, Sodium 1,342.7 mg, Potassium: 1,191.94 mg, Total Carbohydrates: 16.82 g, Protein: 68.39 g

MEATLOAF

SERVINGS: 6

Meatloaf is a traditional meal that is full of flavor. You can use ketchup in this meatloaf, or if you like a slightly spicier version, use barbeque sauce. Serve this meatloaf with corn, green beans or a tossed salad and a side of baked potatoes.

INGREDIENTS

2 eggs
1 1/2 lb. lean ground beef
1 cup onion, finely diced
1/2 cup parsley, finely chopped
3/4 cup rolled oats
3/4 cup ketchup
2 tsp salt
1/2 tsp fresh ground black pepper
2 Tbsp. ketchup

PROCEDURE

1) Beat the eggs into a large bowl.
2) Add the remaining ingredients, except the 2 tablespoons ketchup.
3) Mix well.
4) Form the meatloaf into a casserole dish that will fit in the Instant Pot.
5) Spread the remaining ketchup on top.
6) Place the dish in the instant Pot and cook on high pressure for 15 minutes.
7) Once the pressure releases, check the meatloaf for doneness. It should read 165° F internally.
8) Slice the meatloaf and serve with potatoes and vegetables of choice.

Nutrition Facts: Serving size: 1/6 of a recipe (7.4 ounces). Calories: 408.47, Total Fat: 25.83 g, Cholesterol: 147.05 mg, Sodium: 1,271.52 mg, Total Carbohydrates: 18.71 g, Protein: 24.57 g

PESTO PENNE WITH ARTICHOKE HEARTS

SERVINGS: 3

Using the pressure cooker function makes this meal quick and easy. The delicious flavor of the pesto combined with the tender meat of the artichoke is perfect for a simple and quick dinner.

INGREDIENTS

8 oz. (225 grams) dried pasta (penne, bowtie pasta, fettuccine, etc.)
1 cup cubed fresh or frozen chicken (cut into ¼" cubes, then measure)
6 – 8 tablespoons prepared pesto
1 Tbsp. roasted garlic
1 tsp coarse Kosher salt
¼ tsp coarsely ground pepper
1 cup of artichoke hearts, diced into bite size pieces
Grated parmesan or Romano to garnish (optional)

PROCEDURE

1) Combine 1 cup of water, 1 teaspoon salt and the penne in the Instant Pot. If using frozen chicken, add the chicken to the Instant Pot now.
2) Cook on high pressure for 2 minutes and then use the quick pressure release.
3) Stir the pasta, then drain the extra water. Set the cooker to "keep warm".
4) Add the garlic to the pasta.
5) Add the pesto a spoonful at a time. Thoroughly stir the pesto into the pasta before adding more.
6) Add the chicken now, if you have not already added it.
7) Add the pepper and artichoke heart. Stir the mixture gently.
8) Serve garnished with parmesan or Romano cheese.

Nutrition Facts: Serving size: 1/3 of a recipe (7.8 ounces). Calories: 583.72, Total Fat: 19.79 g, Cholesterol: 56.63 mg, Sodium: 1,071.07 mg, Potassium: 569.24 mg, Total Carbohydrates: 66.56 g, Protein: 34.89 g

RANCH PASTA SALAD

SERVINGS: 8

This pasta salad is quick and easy but full of a delightful summer flavor.

INGREDIENTS

PASTA INGREDIENTS:

16 oz. rotelle or penne pasta
1 tsp coarse kosher salt
2 Tbsp. white wine
1 cup fresh or frozen peas
1 cup diced sweet onion (1/4" dice)
1 cup diced celery
1 cup diced cucumber (1/4" dice) (optional)
2 - 3 cups diced chicken, turkey or ham
¼ cupprecooked Crumbled Bacon
Salt and pepper to taste

DRESSING INGREDIENTS:

½ cupmayonnaise
½ cupsour cream
½ cupbuttermilk
2 garlic cloves, minced
¾ tsp dried chives
¾ tsp dried parsley
½ tsp dried dill
½ tsp onion flakes
½ tsp coarse kosher salt
½ tsp coarsely ground pepper
¼ tsp celery seed

PROCEDURE

1) Combine the pasta, salt, 3 ½ cups water and the wine to the Instant Pot.

2) Cook on high pressure for 2 minutes.
3) Combine the celery, onion and meat.
4) In a separate bowl, combine the dressing ingredients. Mix thoroughly to combine completely and refrigerate until needed.
5) Drain any excess water from the pasta.
6) Add the frozen peas to the pasta now (if using). Once the peas have defrosted, rinse the pasta mixture in cold water to chill it.
7) Add the celery and meat mixture to the pasta and mix to combine.
8) Add half of the dressing and mix to combine. Continue to add dressing a little at a time until the salad reaches a desired consistency.
9) Season to taste with salt and pepper. Sprinkle the bacon on top.
10) Chill until serving.

Nutrition Facts: Serving size: 1/8 of a recipe (9.1 ounces). Calories: 516.25, Total Fat: 14.12 g, Cholesterol: 55.55 mg, Sodium: 652.35 mg, Potassium: 541.83 mg,   Total Carbohydrates: 65.6 g, Protein: 29.38 g

RED BEANS & RICE

SERVINGS: 6

This traditional Spanish meal is packed with flavor and nutrients. The Instant Pot makes quick work of the dried beans. It's a perfect for a quick dinner.

INGREDIENTS

2 Tbsp. oil
1 onion, diced
1 green or red bell pepper, diced
2 – 3 stalks celery, chopped
3 cloves garlic, minced
1 ½ lbs. ham, cut into small cubes
1 lb. dry red kidney beans
1 cup long grain white rice
7 ½ cups water
1 tsp salt
½ tsp black pepper
¼ tsp white pepper
¼ tsp cayenne pepper (or to taste)
½ tsp dried thyme
2 bay leaves

PROCEDURE

1) Sauté the onion, pepper and celery in the oil for 3 minutes.
2) Add the garlic and ham, cooking for an additional 4 minutes.
3) Meanwhile, rinse the beans.
4) Add the remaining ingredients, mix to combine.
5) Bring to high pressure and cook for 40 minutes.
6) Allow the pressure to reduce slowly.

7) Serve immediately.

Nutrition Facts Serving size: 1/6 of a recipe (20.4 ounces). Calories: 334.5, Total Fat: 11.22 g, Cholesterol: 62.37 mg, Sodium: 2,111.08 mg, Potassium: 665.56 mg,   Total Carbohydrates: 23.39 g, Protein: 33.82 g

SEAFOOD GUMBO

SERVINGS: 4

This traditional southern meal is full of flavor. It will quickly become a family favorite.

INGREDIENTS

1 cup long grain white rice
1 ½ cups water
1 cup water
2 ½ cups chicken broth
1 lb. medium shrimp, peeled & deveined
1 lb. sole fillets, cut into 2-inch pieces
1 15 oz. can diced tomatoes
1 medium onion, chopped
2 cups green pepper, chopped
2 cloves garlic, minced
2 bay leaves
1 Tbsp. parsley
1 tsp basil
½ tsp thyme
¼ tsp ground red pepper
¼ tsp salt
¼ cupcold water
2 Tbsp. cornstarch
10 oz. okra, fresh

PROCEDURE

1) Combine the rice with the 1 ½ cups of water in a glass or stainless steel bowl that fits into the cooker bowl.
2) Wrap the bowl the foil, making sure that it is tightly sealed.
3) Place a trivet on the bottom of the Instant Pot. Pour 1 cup of water into the Instant Pot.
4) Place the bowl with the rice on top of the trivet.

5) Cook on low pressure for 15 minutes, then allow the pressure to slowly reduce.
6) Remove the rice and trivet from the cooker.
7) Place the shrimp, broth, tomatoes, onion, green pepper, garlic, bay leaves, parsley, basil, thyme, red pepper and season with salt and pepper.
8) Cook on high pressure for 1 minute. Use the rapid release button to release the pressure quickly.
9) Combine the cornstarch and water in a small bowl. Mix it into the stock, stirring until the sauce thickens.
10) Add the okra and stir the gumbo for 3-4 minutes.
11) Remove the bay leaf before serving over the rice.

Nutrition Facts: Serving size: 1/4 of a recipe (31.7 ounces). Calories: 336.67, Total Fat: 5.35 g, Cholesterol: 206.39 mg, Sodium: 2,031.5 mg, Potassium: 1,044.49 mg, Total Carbohydrates: 32.22 g, Protein: 40.41 g

---

PORK CHOPS IN MUSHROOM GRAVY

SERVINGS: 4

These delicious pork chops are quick and easy to make. They are tender and the mushroom gravy creates a wonderful topping.

INGREDIENTS

> 4 bone-in thick pork chops
> 2 Tbsp. vegetable oil
> 1 1/2 cups water
> 1 can cream of mushroom soup
> 4 Tbsp. water (optional)
> 2 Tbsp. flour (optional)
> Lemon pepper

PROCEDURE

1) Season the pork chops on each side with the lemon pepper, or your seasoning of choice.
2) Sauté the pork chops in the oil until they are evenly browned on each side. You may sauté in either the Instant Pot or a skillet over medium high heat.
3) Once the pork chops are browned, remove them from the pan and add the water to the pan. Heat the water while scraping the bottom and sides of the pan to get all of the seasoning and flavor off.
4) Whisk in the mushroom soup.
5) Return the pork chops to the pot.
6) Cook on high pressure for 18 minutes.
7) If desired, mix together the 4 tablespoons of water and 2 tablespoons of flour until no lumps remain.
8) Use the flour mixture to thicken the gravy to desired consistency.
9) Serve the pork chops with the gravy over the top.

Nutrition Facts: Serving size: 1/4 of a recipe (10 ounces). Calories: 259.02, Total Fat: 14.71 g, Cholesterol: 61.38 mg, Sodium: 584.03 mg, Potassium: 412.4 mg, Total Carbohydrates: 8.1 g, Protein: 22.47 g

SHRIMP PAELLA

SERVINGS: 3

This traditional Spanish dish is served over rice. The flavors of the tomato, garlic, saffron and green beans combine into a mouthwatering dish. Using the pressure cooker makes this quick and easy.

INGREDIENTS

¾ lb. medium size shrimp, peeled and deveined
¼ cuptomato paste or puree
2 cloves garlic, minced
Pinch saffron
1 cup short grain rice
1 ¾ cups hot water
1 cup green beans
2 Tbsp. olive oil

PROCEDURE

1) Sauté the garlic and saffron in the pot using the sauté mode. Cook for 2 minutes.
2) Add the rice and green beans. Cook for 3 minutes.
3) Add the liquid and cook on high pressure for 8 minutes.
4) Rapidly release the pressure and add the shrimp.
5) Cook on high pressure for an additional minute. Rapidly release the pressure and serve hot.

Nutrition Facts: Serving size: 1/3 of a recipe (14 ounces). Calories: 271.83, Total Fat: 10.43 g, Cholesterol: 142.88 mg, Sodium: 820.05 mg, Potassium: 431.14 mg, Total Carbohydrates: 25.94 g, Protein: 18.56 g

SLOW-COOKER CORNED BEEF AND CABBAGE

SERVINGS: 6

This is a simple and delicious way to prepare a traditional meal. The salty and rich flavor of the corned beef is perfectly complemented by the subtle cabbage.

INGREDIENTS

2 celery stalks, cut into 3-inch pieces
3 carrots, cut into 3-inch pieces
1 small yellow onion, cut into 1-inch wedges (root end left intact)
1/2 lb.   small potatoes, halved if large
6 sprigs thyme
1 corned beef brisket (about 3 pounds), plus pickling spice packet or 1 tablespoon pickling spice
1/2 head Savoy cabbage, cut into 1 1/2-inch wedges
Grainy mustard, for serving

PROCEDURE

1) Place the celery, carrots, onions, potatoes and thyme in the Instant Pot.
2) Add the corned beef on top of the vegetables, being sure to place the fat side up.
3) Add enough water to the pot to cover the vegetables.
4) Cook on high for 4 - 5 hours, or low for 7 - 8 hours.
5) Carefully arrange the cabbage over the corned beef. Continue to cook until the cabbage is tender, about 1 1/2 hours on low and 45 minutes on high.
6) Remove all the vegetables and corned beef from the pot.
7) Thinly slice the corned beef against the grain and arrange on a large platter. Arrange the vegetables around the corned beef.

8) Serve hot.

Nutrition Facts: Serving size: 1/6 of a recipe (12.5 ounces). Calories: 508.89, Total Fat: 34.02 g, Cholesterol:122.47 mg, Sodium: 2,845 mg, Potassium: 1,054.6 mg, Total Carbohydrates: 13.87 g, Protein: 35.02 g

SOY-CITRUS CHICKEN

SERVINGS: 4

These delicious chicken thighs are tender and moist. Topped with a slightly spicy citrus flavored sauce that goes well with a side of rice.

INGREDIENTS

1 orange, halved and thinly sliced
1 1/2 lbs. skinless, boneless chicken thighs (5 to 6 thighs)
1 Tbsp. all-purpose flour
1/2 tsp grated lemon zest
Kosher salt and freshly ground pepper
1/2 cup sweet chili sauce
1 Tbsp. low-sodium soy sauce
1 1-inch piece ginger, peeled and minced
3 cloves garlic, minced
6 oz. thin rice noodles
1 bunch watercress, tough stems removed, coarsely chopped
1 Tbsp. chopped fresh cilantro

PROCEDURE

1) On the bottom of the Instant Pot bowl, layer the orange slices in a single layer.
2) In a bowl, combine the flour, lemon zest, 1/4 teaspoon salt and a pinch of pepper. Season the chicken with the flour mixture.
3) Add the seasoned chicken to the Instant Pot in a single layer on top of the oranges.
4) Combine the chili sauce, soy sauce, ginger and garlic. Pour over the chicken.
5) Cook on the slow cooker setting on low for 7 hours. Then gently stir, making sure to break up the chicken so that it's in evenly sized pieces.
6) Let the chicken stand for 10 minutes.
7) Meanwhile, cook the noodles according to package directions. Drain the noodles and toss in a large bowl with the watercress.

8) Serve the chicken mixture over the top of the noodles and garnish with cilantro.

Nutrition Facts: Serving size: 1/4 of a recipe (4.6 ounces). Calories: 125.15, Total Fat: 0.88 g, Cholesterol: 12.76 mg, Sodium: 164.37 mg, Potassium: 243.76 mg,   Total Carbohydrates: 25.79 g, Protein: 5.09 g

---

STUFFED TURKEY BREAST ROLL

SERVINGS: 8

This turkey breast roll is delicious. It's simple and easy to make but presents an elegant meal.

INGREDIENTS

> 2 Tbsp. un-salted butter
> 2 celery stalks, chopped
> 2 small red onions, chopped
> 2 cloves garlic, minced
> 2 sprigs fresh sage, chopped (about 2 tablespoons)
> 1 ½ tsp salt, divided
> 1 pinch pepper
> 2 cups (200g) plain dried breadcrumbs
> 1 cup (250ml) whole milk
> A few springs parsley, chopped (about 2 tablespoons)
> 1 Tbsp. olive oil
> 2 ½ -3 lb. (1 - 1.5k) boneless & skinless turkey breast, butterflied (sliced so that it is suitable for rolling) and pounded to an even thickness
> 2 tsp grainy mustard
> 2 cups (500ml) vegetable stock

PROCEDURE

1) Sauté the onions, celery, garlic and sage in butter until the vegetables have softened.
2) Meanwhile, combine the breadcrumbs, 1 teaspoon salt and parsley in a medium bowl. Mix well.
3) Add the milk to the breadcrumb mixture and mix until the milk is well mixed in.
4) Add the sautéed vegetables to the breadcrumb mixture and set aside.
5) Season the turkey breast with salt and pepper.

6) Spread an even layer of the breadcrumb mixture over the turkey breast, but be sure to leave ½-inch bare on all the sides.
7) Roll the turkey breast and secure with twine.
8) Place the rolled turkey breast in the Instant Pot with the olive oil. Brown the turkey breast evenly on all sides.
9) Once the turkey breast is browned, rub the mustard evenly over the surface.
10) Cook on high pressure for 20 – 25 minutes.
11) Remove the turkey breast from the cooker and slice into 1-inch thick slices.
12) Serve the turkey garnished with cranberry sauce and drizzle a little of the cooking liquid over the top.

Nutrition Facts: Serving size: 1/8 of a recipe (10.9 ounces). Calories: 345.87, Total Fat: 9.8 g, Cholesterol: 68.27 mg, Sodium: 2,200.63 mg, Potassium: 624.31 mg, Total Carbohydrates: 32.12 g, Protein: 30.9 g

TERIYAKI CHICKEN

SERVINGS: 6

This delicious and moist chicken is tender and quick to make. The sauce is rich and flavorful. Teriyaki chicken goes well with a side of rice and stir fry vegetables or an Asian cucumber salad.

INGREDIENTS

> *2 lbs. boneless chicken breasts*
> *1/2 cup soy sauce*
> *1/2 cup water*
> *1/2 cup white, granulated sugar*
> *1/2 tsp ground ginger*
> *1 Tbsp. cornstarch*

PROCEDURE

1) Combine the soy sauce, water, sugar, ginger and garlic in a small saucepan. Bring to a boil, then reduce heat and cook for 3 – 5 minutes.
2) Layer the chicken into the Instant Pot and pour the sauce over the chicken.
3) Cook on low pressure for 20 minutes.
4) Meanwhile, mix the cornstarch and water.
5) Once the chicken is done cooking, allow the pressure to reduce and then use the rapid release.
6) Add the cornstarch mixture and stir it in to thicken. You may need to turn on sauté for 1 – 2 minutes to make sure the sauce is boiling and the cornstarch will thicken the mixture.

7) Serve the chicken hot, topped with the sauce and served with a side of rice and vegetables.

Nutrition Facts: Serving size: 1/6 of a recipe (2.7 ounces). Calories: 101.23, Total Fat: 0.43 g, Cholesterol: 8.51 mg, Sodium: 718.59 mg, Potassium: 71.3 mg, Total Carbohydrates: 21.6 g, Protein: 3.25 g

SMOKEY BEEF BRISKET

SERVINGS: 6

This beef brisket turns out tender every time - in an hour. Serve with scalloped potatoes and a tossed salad or baked potatoes and carrots.

INGREDIENTS

2 lb. beef brisket, flat cut, fat trimmed
1 tsp seasoned meat tenderizer
1/4 tsp celery salt
1/4 tsp seasoned salt
1/4 tsp garlic salt
2 Tbsp. liquid smoke
1 Tbsp. Worcester sauce
1/2 cup water
1 cup BBQ sauce, plus additional for serving

PROCEDURE

1) In a small bowl, combine the tenderizer, celery salt, seasoned salt and garlic salt. Season the brisket with the combined spices.
2) In a large resealable bag, combine the brisket with the liquid smoke and Worcestershire sauce.
3) Marinate the brisket overnight.
4) Combine the water and barbeque sauce in the Instant Pot.
5) Add the contents of the bag.
6) Cook on high pressure for 60 minutes.
7) Remove the meat from the pot and slice across the grain.
8) Serve the meat with additional barbeque sauce (if desired).

Nutrition Facts: Serving size: 1/6 of a recipe (8.3 ounces). Calories: 237.86, Total Fat: 8.72 g, Cholesterol: 101.3 mg, Sodium: 526.49 mg, Potassium: 823.98 mg,   Total Carbohydrates: 6.56 g, Protein: 33.42 g

---

4

SIDE DISHES

"Baked" Sweet Potatoes

Servings: 4

These sweet potatoes are moist, tender and quick to make with the Instant Pot.

Ingredients

> 2-3 large sweet potatoes
> ½ cupwater
> Tad of extra virgin olive oil

Procedure

1) Wash the potatoes and brush with olive oil.
2) Wrap the potatoes in foil.
3) Add ½ cup water to the Instant Pot and place a trivet into the pot.
4) Place the potatoes on top of the trivet and steam for 75 minutes.
5) Remove the potatoes and the foil from the potatoes.
6) Add toppings and serve.
7) Suggested toppings: sour cream, Greek yogurt, walnuts, ground flax, miniature marshmallows, cream cheese, etc.

Nutrition Facts: Serving size: 1/4 of a recipe (4.6 ounces). Calories: 83.85, Total Fat: 0.05 g, Cholesterol: 0 mg, Sodium: 54.51 mg, Potassium: 328.87 mg, Total Carbohydrates: 19.62 g, Protein: 1.53 g

---

BUTTERNUT SQUASH RISOTTO

SERVINGS: 6

This delicious creamy rice dish takes on a fall twist with the addition of butternut squash. The squash adds color and a tasty nutty flavor to the rice.

INGREDIENTS

> *2 Tbsp. olive oil*
> *2 Tbsp. butter*
> *1 white onion, diced*
> *2 cups Arborio rice*
> *2 cups butternut squash, cubed into 1 inch pieces*
> *6 cups chicken broth*
> *¾ cupdry, white wine*
> *1 cinnamon stick*
> *1 ½ Tbsp. fresh basil, chopped*
> *3 Tbsp. Romano cheese, grated*
> *Sea salt & fresh ground black pepper to taste*

PROCEDURE

1) Sauté the onion in the butter and oil.
2) Add the squash and cook for 3 – 4 minutes.
3) Add the rice and cook for another 2 minutes.
4) Add the wine and mix to combine. Cook for 2 minutes.
5) Add the broth, basil and cinnamon stick. Cook on high pressure for 15 minutes.
6) Quick release the pressure and fold in the cheese. Replace the lid for 1 minute.
7) The rice should be creamy, if it's too dry, add more broth.
8) Serve hot.

Nutrition Facts: Serving size: 1/6 of a recipe (14.6 ounces). Calories: 407.17, Total Fat: 10.87 g, Cholesterol: 11 mg, Sodium: 884.33 mg, Potassium: 432.3 mg, Total Carbohydrates: 60.53 g, Protein: 10.38 g

---

CHEESY POTATOES AU GRATIN

SERVINGS: 6

Au gratin potatoes are a delicious side to any meal. These savory, cheesy potatoes are perfect to go with meatloaf, chicken, prime rib, steaks, or pork.

INGREDIENTS

2 Tbsp. butter
1/2 cup chopped onion
1 cup chicken broth
6 medium sized potatoes peeled and sliced 1/8 inch thick
1/2 tsp salt
1/8 tsp pepper
1/2 cup sour cream
1 cup shredded Monterey jack cheese
Topping
3 Tbsp. butter, melted
1 cup panko bread crumbs

PROCEDURE

1) In the Instant pot, sauté the onion in butter until the onion is tender.
2) Add 1 cup of chicken broth, salt and pepper.
3) Place the steamer basket in the pot and add the potatoes to the basket.
4) Cook on high pressure for 5 minutes.
5) Meanwhile, preheat the broiler.
6) Mix together the breadcrumbs and melted butter. Set aside.
7) Once the Instant Pot is done cooking, use the quick pressure release. Remove the potatoes and carefully place in a greased 9x13 inch pan.
8) Combine the sour cream and cheese with the liquid remaining in the cooker.
9) Pour over the potatoes and gently mix to coat the potatoes.

10) Sprinkle on the breadcrumbs. Broil for 5 – 7 minutes, or until the top is golden brown.

Nutrition Facts: Serving size: 1/6 of a recipe (10.8 ounces). Calories: 416.71, Total Fat: 20.44 g, Cholesterol: 52.17 mg, Sodium: 577.11 mg, Potassium: 909.53 mg,   Total Carbohydrates: 47.21 g, Protein: 12.19 g

CANDIED YAMS

SERVINGS: 4

These yams are simple but full of flavor. The butter, brown sugar and orange juice add incredible flavor to the sweet potatoes. This is a perfect fall dish to go along with a roast of beef.

INGREDIENTS

1 cup orange juice
2 large sweet potatoes, chopped
Salt to taste
½ cupbrown sugar
1 tsp orange zest
2 Tbsp. butter

PROCEDURE

1) Combine all the ingredients in the cooker.
2) Cook on high for 7 minutes.
3) Rapidly release the pressure.
4) Remove the potatoes from the cooker, leaving the sauce.
5) Reduce the sauce until it thickens. Return the potatoes to the cooker and toss to coat.
6) Serve immediately. Optional, garnish with pecans.

Nutrition Facts: Serving size: 1/4 of a recipe (8.7 ounces). Calories: 360.79, Total Fat: 6.14 g, Cholesterol: 15.27 mg, Sodium: 95.29 mg, Potassium:1,387.35 mg,   Total Carbohydrates: 75.37 g, Protein: 2.83 g

CORN & RICE SALAD

SERVINGS: 4

This salad is full of color and flavor. It goes well with grilled chicken a grilled pork chop.

INGREDIENTS

1 cup wild rice blend
2 cups water
½ tsp salt
2 Tbsp. olive oil, divided
1 medium leek
1 clove garlic, minced
2 Tbsp. pine nuts or sliced almonds
1 cup corn kernels
½ cupdried blueberries
1 Tbsp. flat leaf parsley, chopped
½ Tbsp. chives, chopped

PROCEDURE

1) Combine the rice, water and 1 tsp of olive oil in the Instant Pot. Cook on low pressure for 20 minutes.
2) Slowly release pressure.
3) While the pressure is reducing, trim the leek and cut into thin slices.
4) Remove the rice from the cooker and add 1 Tbsp. of olive oil.
5) Sauté the leek for 2 minutes, then add the garlic and cook for an additional minute.
6) Add the remaining ingredients and cook for 3 minutes.
7) Add the rice and stir to combine.
8) Serve immediately.

Nutrition Facts: Serving size: 1/4 of a recipe (9 ounces). Calories: 286.54, Total Fat: 9.84 g, Cholesterol: 0 mg, Sodium: 404.2 mg, Potassium: 357.05 mg, Total Carbohydrate: 44.76 g, Protein: 8.44 g

---

CRISPY POTATOES

SERVINGS: 4

These potatoes are tender and moist. They go well with meatloaf, grilled chicken, steak or salmon seasoned with lemon and dill.

INGREDIENTS

4 medium potatoes, cut into ½-inch strips
Salt & Pepper to taste
¾ cupchicken or vegetable stock
For Topping:
2 Tbsp. butter
2 Tbsp. onion, minced
1 clove garlic, minced
½ cup bread crumbs
¼ tsp dried basil
¼ tsp thyme
1 Tbsp. dried parsley
¼ tsp paprika

PROCEDURE

1) Mix together the topping ingredients, set aside.
2) Melt the butter on the sauté mode, and sauté the onions and garlic for 4 – 5 minutes, or until the onion becomes translucent.
3) Add the topping mixture to the cooker and stir until well combined. Cook for 2 minutes, or until lightly browned.
4) Remove from the cooker.
5) In a steamer basket, layer the potato strips and season each layer.
6) Place the basket in the cooker, and add 1 cup water.
7) Cook on high for 4 minutes.
8) Use the rapid release to rapidly release the pressure.
9) Remove the potatoes from the steamer basket and place the potatoes in a serving bowl.

10) Add the toppings and serve.

Nutrition Facts: Serving size: 1/4 of a recipe (9.1 ounces). Calories: 266.42, Total Fat: 7.22 g, Cholesterol: 176.06 mg, Sodium: 176.06 mg, Potassium: 871.92 mg,   Total Carbohydrates: 44.41 g, Protein: 6.89 g

CURRIED QUINOA

SERVINGS: 4

This gluten free curried quinoa is packed with flavor and nutrients. The leftovers of this make a perfect lunch. They're quick and easy to heat up and are even more delicious the next day.

INGREDIENTS

1 pinch saffron threads
1/2 cup warm water
1 cup quinoa
1 cup chickpeas, cooked
½ cup raisins
1 small eggplant, cubed
1 small squash, cubed
1 small sweet potato, cubed
½ cup green beans
½ cup onions, diced
½ hot pepper, sliced (optional)
5 oz. coconut milk
1 tsp cumin seeds
1 Tbsp. butter
6 whole cloves
2/3 tsp Madras curry powder
1/3 tsp curry powder
1/3 tsp garam masala

PROCEDURE

1) Soak the saffron seeds in the water for 5 minutes.
2) Combine the saffron and water, quinoa, chickpeas and raisins in the cooker.
3) Place the vegetables in a steamer basket on top of the quinoa. You may use a trivet on top of the quinoa. Layer the vegetables with the squash and sweet potatoes on the bottom. Next place the pepper,

then the eggplant with the beans on the top. This will allow the vegetables to cook properly without overcooking.

4) Cook on high pressure for 5-6 minutes.
5) Meanwhile, melt the butter in a small pan and fry the cumin seeds for 2 – 3 minutes. Add the onions and sauté for an additional 3 minutes.
6) Add the milk to the mixture and the remaining spices. Cook for about 10 minutes, or until the sauce begins to thicken.
7) Remove the vegetables from the cooker and coat in the curry sauce.
8) Serve the quinoa topped with the curry vegetables.

Nutrition Facts: Serving size: 1/4 of a recipe (15.2 ounces). Calories: 469.39, Total Fat: 14.42 g, Cholesterol: 7.63 mg, Sodium: 218.5 mg, Potassium: 1,165.97 mg, Total Carbohydrates: 77.76 g, Protein: 13.14 g

---

GARLIC VEGETABLES

SERVINGS: 4

These vegetables are tender and moist. The garlic and bay leaf add richness to the dish. They are the perfect side to nearly any meal. Pair these vegetables with beef roasts, grilled chicken breasts or pork loins.

INGREDIENTS

4 – 6 cloves garlic, minced
Salt & Pepper to taste
2 Tbsp. vegetable oil
¼ cup water or chicken broth
1 bay leaf
1 medium onion, quartered
3 carrots, sliced
2 celery stalks, sliced
3 medium potatoes, cut into quarters (russet, Yukon or red potatoes)

PROCEDURE

1) Sauté the onions and garlic for 4 – 5 minutes, or until the onions are translucent.
2) Add the remaining ingredients. Cook on low for 10 minutes.
3) Release the pressure slowly.
4) Serve immediately.

Nutrition Facts: Serving size: 1/4 of a recipe (9.8 ounces). Calories: 215.8, Total Fat: 7.44 g, Cholesterol: 0 mg, Sodium: 186.27 mg, Potassium: 903.3 mg, Total Carbohydrates: 34.51 g, Protein: 4.34 g

---

GREEN BEANS & POTATOES

SERVINGS: 4

This dish is simple and easy to make, but it's tasty. If you'd like to dress it up a bit, just sprinkle some French fried onions on top before serving.

INGREDIENTS

3 potatoes, peeled and cut into 1-inch cubes
¾ lb. green beans
1 Tbsp. olive oil
1 medium onion, thinly sliced
1 clove garlic, minced
1 green pepper, diced
1 Tbsp. parsley, minced
Salt & Pepper to taste
½ cup chicken stock

PROCEDURE

1) Sauté the onion and garlic in the olive oil for 3 minutes.
2) Add the remaining ingredients and cook on high pressure for 3 minutes.
3) Allow the pressure to slowly release.
4) Serve hot.

Nutrition Facts: Serving size: 1/4 of a recipe (11.5 ounces). Calories: 178.85, Total Fat: 3.86 g, Cholesterol: 0 mg, Sodium: 175.32 mg, Potassium: 815.9 mg, Total Carbohydrates: 32.9 g, Protein: 5.1 g

HOT POTATO SALAD

SERVINGS: 4

This potato salad is a type of traditional German potato salad. It doesn't have mayonnaise, like American potato salads, instead it has vinegar which adds a truly delicious zing to the potatoes.

INGREDIENTS

> *4 slices bacon, chopped into ¼" pieces*
> *4 tsp sugar*
> *3 Tbsp. distilled vinegar*
> *1 tsp mustard*
> *4 medium or large potatoes, cut into thin slices*
> *1 medium onion, thinly sliced*
> *Salt & Pepper to taste*
> *½ tsp celery seed*

PROCEDURE

1) Cook the bacon on the sauté setting until it's crispy.
2) Remove the bacon and drain on a paper towel.
3) Reserve 1 tsp of oil, but discard any additional oil.
4) In a small bowl, mix together the sugar, vinegar, mustard and reserved bacon grease.
5) Add 1 ¾ cups water into the cooker.
6) Place the onions and potatoes into a steamer basket. Place the basket in the cooker.
7) Cook on high pressure for 8 – 10 minutes.
8) Rapidly release the pressure, then remove the potatoes and onions from the cooker.
9) Add the vinegar mixture and toss to coat.
10) Serve hot.

Nutrition Facts: Serving size: 1/4 of a recipe (9.5 ounces). Calories: 348.14, Total Fat: 17.42 g, Cholesterol: 25.84 mg, Sodium: 414.83 mg, Potassium: 907.97 mg, Total Carbohydrates: 39.65 g, Protein: 8.57 g

---

JEERA RICE

SERVINGS: 4

This rice is distinctly Indian. It's not overly spicy, but is full of aromatic flavors. It's perfect alongside chicken satay with peanut sauce.

INGREDIENTS

1 cup Basmati rice
1 medium onion, finely chopped
3 tsp butter
1 Tbsp. Jerra (cumin) seeds
½ tsp Garam masala
2 cloves
1 piece of cinnamon, 1 inch long
1 bay leaf
1 star anise, optional

PROCEDURE

1) Rinse the rice and then soak for 20 minutes. Discard the soaking water.
2) Melt the butter on the sauté mode and sauté the onions for 2 minutes. Add the cloves, cinnamon, bay leaf and jeera seeds. Cook for 1 minute.
3) Add the rice and sauté for an additional 2 minutes.
4) Add the hot water and cook on the rice function.
5) Serve hot.

Nutrition Facts: Serving size: 1/4 of a recipe (2.7 ounces). Calories: 102.25, Total Fat: 3.68 g, Cholesterol: 7.63 mg, Sodium: 7.42 mg, Potassium: 111.18 mg, Total Carbohydrates: 16.29 g, Protein: 1.9 g

INDIAN RICE

SERVINGS: 6

This rice is full of flavor and is a perfect side to curry or satay. It's simple and quick but delicious.

INGREDIENTS

2 cups long grain rice
4 cups water
2 tsp salt
2 cloves
2 cardamom pods
1 cinnamon stick
3 Tbsp. vegetable oil
½ tsp dark mustard seeds
½ tsp cumin seeds
¼ tsp chili flakes
1 medium onion, chopped
3 cloves garlic, minced
¼ tsp turmeric

PROCEDURE

1) Wash the rice several times and then soak for 30 minutes.
2) Combine the rice, water, cloves, cinnamon and cardamom.
3) Cook on high pressure for 10 minutes.
4) Remove the rice and remove the spices from the rice. Set the rice aside.
5) Add the oil, mustard, cumin and chili.
6) Cook for 1 minute on sauté.
7) Add the onion and cook until it turns golden brown.
8) Add the garlic and cook for an additional 2 minutes.
9) Add the rice back and the turmeric.
10) Cook for an additional 3 minutes then serve hot.

Nutrition Facts: Serving size: 1/6 of a recipe (8.7 ounces). Calories: 153.13, Total Fat: 7.56 g, Cholesterol: 0 mg, Sodium: 786.11 mg, Potassium: 79.98 mg, Total Carbohydrates: 20.17 g, Protein: 2.03 g

MUSHROOM & PARSLEY POTATOES

SERVINGS: 4

These potatoes are simple, but are incredibly tasty with the sautéed mushrooms and onions.

INGREDIENTS

> 1 Tbsp. olive oil
> ¼ lb. fresh mushrooms, trimmed and sliced
> ½ cup onion, finely chopped
> Salt & freshly ground pepper, to taste
> ½ cupchicken or vegetable stock
> 4 cups potatoes, ½-inch slices
> 2 Tbsp. dried parsley

PROCEDURE

1) Sauté the onions and mushrooms in the oil.
2) Add the remaining ingredients and cook on high pressure for 3 minutes.
3) Use the rapid release to quickly release the pressure.
4) Serve hot.

Nutrition Facts: Serving size: 1/4 of a recipe (19 ounces). Calories: 404.83, Total Fat: 4.27 g, Cholesterol: 0.9 mg, Sodium: 73.47 mg, Potassium: 2,071.07 mg, Total Carbohydrates: 83.22 g, Protein: 11.07 g

---

RATATOUILLE

SERVINGS: 4

Ratatouille is a tasty and healthy way to prepare vegetables. It's a great way to use some of those garden vegetables in the summer.

INGREDIENTS

3 Tbsp. olive oil
1 onion, chopped
2 cloves garlic, minced
1 red bell pepper, diced
1 zucchini, diced
15 oz. tomatoes, diced
¼ cup water
1 tsp salt
Fresh ground black pepper
1 large eggplant, diced
2 Tbsp. fresh basil, minced
2 Tbsp. flat leaf Italian parsley, minced
2 Tbsp. red wine vinegar

PROCEDURE

1) Sauté the onions, garlic and bell pepper in the olive oil until the onion is translucent.
2) Add the zucchini, tomatoes and eggplant. Cook for an additional 2 minutes.
3) Add the water and cook on low pressure for 4 minutes.
4) Allow the pressure to slowly release and then add the basil and parsley. Mix well.
5) Add the vinegar and mix well.
6) Serve hot.

Nutrition Facts: Serving size: 1/4 of a recipe (13.4 ounces). Calories: 178.44, Total Fat: 10.97 g, Cholesterol: 0 mg, Sodium: 600.09 mg, Potassium: 842.24 mg, Total Carbohydrates: 19.15 g, Protein: 4.11 g

---

SEARED MARINATED ARTICHOKES

SERVINGS: 6

These succulent and savory artichokes are a perfect side. They add flavor, color and nutrients to your meal.

INGREDIENTS

4 large artichokes
2 Tbsp. fresh lemon juice
2 tsp balsamic vinegar
¼ cup olive oil
1 tsp dried oregano
2 cloves garlic, minced fine
½ tsp sea salt
¼ tsp fresh ground black pepper

PROCEDURE

1) Wash and clean the artichokes by cutting the stems to ½ inch and remove the lower petals that are tough. Cut off the top inch of the artichoke and remove any thorny tips of the petals with a pair of kitchen shears.
2) Place the artichokes in the steamer basket and place it in the Instant Pot. Add 2 cups of water.
3) Steam for 8 minutes.
4) Meanwhile, prepare the marinade. Combine the lemon juice, balsamic vinegar, olive oil, oregano, garlic, salt and pepper in a jar and tightly fit the lid on it. Shake the jar until the marinade is emulsified.
5) Remove the artichokes when the cooking is complete and allow them to cool.
6) Slice the artichokes in half and remove the center leaves that are purple. Remove the fuzz covering the artichoke heart.
7) Drizzle the marinade over the artichokes, tossing to coat well. Marinate for 30 minutes or overnight.

8) Before serving, sear the artichokes for 3 – 5 minutes. Serve immediately after searing

---

Nutrition Facts: Serving size: 1/6 of a recipe (4.4 ounces). Calories: 135.45, Total Fat: 9.19 g, Cholesterol: 0 mg, Sodium: 130.89 mg, Potassium: 415.23 mg,   Total Carbohydrates: 12.57 g, Protein: 3.66 g

---

QUINOA SALAD

SERVINGS: 4

Quinoa is cooked just like rice, but has a more seed like and nutty texture and flavor. It goes well in salads and pilafs. This salad is light and fresh. It's a breath of summer in your meal.

INGREDIENTS

½ cupwhite quinoa – rinsed for 30 seconds in cold water (using strainer)
1 cup water
½ cupblack beans
3 cups water
4 of the mini cucumbers sliced or diced
1 hot pepper seeded and diced
1/2 green pepper diced – optional or use red pepper
Feta cheese – cubed, as much or as little as you like
¼ diced Purple onion –or use a couple of green onions cut up
1 can of cooked corn
1 cup tomatoes

DRESSING:

½ cupoil
½ cupcitrus juice (lemon or lime)
1 tsp ground cumin
4 – 5 sprigs of flat leaf parsley
4 – 5 leaves mint
4 – 5 leaves basil (optional)
Salt & pepper to taste

PROCEDURE

1) Place the quinoa and 1 cup water in the Instant Pot. Cook on high pressure for 2 minutes.
2) Remove the quinoa and fluff. Set it aside.

3) Place the beans and 3 cups water in the pot and cook on high pressure for 20 minutes.
4) Drain the beans and set aside.
5) In a bowl, combine the cucumbers, peppers, corn and tomatoes.
6) Add the quinoa and beans. Toss to combine.
7) In a blender or food processor combine the dressing ingredients until smooth.
8) Pour the dressing over the salad and toss to mix well.
9) Serve chilled.

Nutrition Facts: Serving size: 1/4 of a recipe (21.8 ounces). Calories: 433.97, Total Fat: 29.72 g, Cholesterol: 0 mg, Sodium: 147.9 mg, Potassium: 748.55 mg, Total Carbohydrates: 37.76 g, Protein: 8.56 g

---

SEASONED ROOT VEGETABLES

SERVINGS: 4

These vegetables are glazed with a ginger and sugar sauce. They are tender and succulent, a perfect side to nearly any meal.

INGREDIENTS

2 Tbsp. brown sugar
2 tsp ground ginger
1/2 cup water, optional
2 Tbsp. cornstarch, optional
Salt & Pepper to taste
2 Tbsp. butter
1 medium onion, thinly sliced
2 cloves garlic, minced
2 medium turnips, peeled and cut into chunks
3 carrots, chopped
2 medium parsnips, peeled and sliced ½-inch thick
1 cup chicken broth

PROCEDURE

1) Melt the butter on sauté mode and sauté the onions and garlic for 3 minutes.
2) Add the turnips and carrots and cook for another 3 minutes.
3) Add the parsnips, broth, ginger and sugar.
4) Cook on high pressure for 1 minutes.
5) Quickly release pressure.
6) While the pressure releases, mix the cornstarch and water together (if using).
7) Thicken the sauce with the cornstarch mixture.

8) Serve hot.

Nutrition Facts: Serving size: 1/4 of a recipe (15 ounces). Calories: 267.75, Total Fat: 6.79 g, Cholesterol: 15.27 mg, Sodium: 176.17 mg, Potassium: 987.14 mg, Total Carbohydrates: 49.87 g, Protein: 4.73 g

STEAMED BROCCOLI

SERVINGS: 6

Broccoli is a classic vegetable that is tender and flavorful. When lightly steamed, it's perfect to add color and texture to your meal.

INGREDIENTS

> *2 heads broccoli, cut into florets*
> *½ cupwater*
> *1 tsp sea salt*

PROCEDURE

1) Place all ingredients into the Instant Pot and cook on high for 3-4 minutes.
2) Serve hot.

Nutrition Facts: Serving size: 1/6 of a recipe (4.2 ounces). Calories: 37.15, Total Fat: 0.57 g, Cholesterol: 0 mg, Potassium: 307.86 mg, Total Carbohydrates: 6.56 g, Protein: 3.06 g

---

SWEET CARROTS

SERVINGS: 4

These glazed carrots are sweet and colorful. They cook quickly in the Instant Pot, the end result being tender and moist.

INGREDIENTS

1/2 Tbsp. butter
1 Tbsp. brown sugar
1/2 cup water
Pinch of salt
2 cups baby carrots

PROCEDURE

1) Combine the butter, sugar, water and salt in the Instant Pot.
2) Stir the mixture while the pot is on sauté until the butter is melted.
3) Add the carrots and stir to coat the carrots with the mixture.
4) Steam the carrots for 15 minutes.
5) Once the time is up, sauté the carrots until the liquid is gone.
6) Serve hot.

Nutrition Facts: Serving size: 1/4 of a recipe (3.2 ounces). Calories: 45.63, Total Fat: 1.51 g, Cholesterol: 3.82 mg, Sodium: 118.94 mg, Potassium: 139.69 mg, Total Carbohydrates: 8.04 g, Protein: 0.38 g

TAWA PULAO

SERVINGS: 6

This delicious Indian street food is colorful and packed with flavor.

INGREDIENTS

> 3 cups cooked rice
> ½ cupgreen beans
> ½ cupcarrot, chopped
> 2 Tbsp. butter
> 1 tsp cumin seeds
> ½ tsp ginger paste
> ½ tsp garlic paste
> 3 green chilies, chopped
> ½ cup onion, finely chopped
> ½ cupgreen pepper, chopped
> 1 ¼ cups tomatoes, chopped
> ¼ tsp turmeric powder
> 2 tsp red chili powder
> 4 tsp Pav Bhaji masala
> ¼ cupwater
> 1 Tbsp. Lemon juice
> Salt to taste

PROCEDURE

1) Sauté the beans, carrots and cumin seeds in the butter. Cook until the seeds become fragrant.
2) Add the ginger paste, garlic paste and green chili. Cook for one minute.
3) Add the onions and cook until the onions are translucent.
4) Add the remaining ingredients – except lemon juice - and cook on low pressure for 3 minutes.
5) Quickly release pressure and add the lemon juice.

6) Serve immediately.

Nutrition Facts: Serving size: 1/6 of a recipe (13.1 ounces). Calories: 192.58, Total Fat: 4.49 g, Cholesterol: 10.18 mg, Sodium: 779.88 mg, Potassium: 442.84 mg, Total Carbohydrates: 35.28 g, Protein: 4.54 g

VEGETABLE BIRYANI

SERVINGS: 4

Biryani is a traditional Indian vegetable medley that is often served with mint chutney. It's flavorful, colorful and delicious.

INGREDIENTS

1 ½ cups basmati rice
1 potato, cubed
1 carrot, chopped
½ cupgreen peas
1 onion, sliced
1 Tbsp. ginger garlic paste
2 Tbsp. mint leaves, chopped
1– 2 green chilies
1 Tbsp. lemon juice
2 ½ tsp Biryani Masala Powder
2 ½ cups water
3 Tbsp. oil
1 bay leaf
4 green cardamoms
1 star anise
2 cinnamon sticks (2 inches long each)
½ tsp shahi jeera

PROCEDURE

1) Sauté the vegetables in the oil for 3 – 4 minutes.
2) Add the rice and seasonings and stir. Cook for 2 minutes.
3) Add the garlic ginger paste and mint leave. Cook for another 2 minutes.
4) Add the water, biryani masala and lemon juice.
5) Cook on high pressure for 10 minutes.
6) Allow the pressure to slowly release.

7) Stir the rice and serve hot.

Nutrition Facts: Serving size: 1/4 of a recipe (12.4 ounces). Calories: 267.99, Total Fat: 11 g, Cholesterol: 0 mg, Sodium: 61.38 mg, Potassium: 412.07 mg,   Total Carbohydrates: 40.41 g, Protein: 4.69 g

---

VEGETABLE MEDLEY

SERVINGS: 6

This is a great way to use fresh garden vegetables in the summer. It's colorful, fresh and full of delicious flavor.

INGREDIENTS

1 medium onion, chopped
2 Tbsp. canola oil
¾ cupred split lentils
1 clove garlic, minced
¼ cupparsley, minced
¼ cupfresh dill, minced or 1 Tbsp. dried dill
1 tsp fresh basil, minced
1 cup chicken or vegetable stock
3 large tomatoes, chopped small
2 zucchini, cut into thin slices
4 medium potatoes, cut into ½" slices
2 large carrots, cut into ½" slices
1 green pepper, diced
2 stalks celery, sliced
2 cups peas
Salt & Pepper to taste

PROCEDURE

1) Sauté the onions in the oil until translucent. Add the garlic, parsley and dill to the onions. Continue to cook for 1 minute.
2) Add the remaining ingredients. Mix well.
3) Cook on high pressure for 5 minutes.
4) Use the rapid release button to rapidly reduce the pressure.
5) Serve hot.

Nutrition Facts: Serving size: 1/6 of a recipe (23.2 ounces). Calories: 414.13, Total Fat: 7.21 g, Cholesterol: 1.2 mg, Sodium: 720.13 mg, Potassium: 1,818.84 mg,   Total Carbohydrates: 74.2 g, Protein: 17.6 g

---

5

SOUPS

BEAN AND BARLEY SOUP

SERVINGS: 8

This delicious soup is perfect for a busy day. Simply put everything in the Instant Pot in the morning and when it's evening - you'll have dinner ready to go.

INGREDIENTS

1 cup dried Great Northern beans
1/2 cup pearl barley
3 cloves garlic, smashed
2 medium carrots, roughly chopped
2 ribs celery, roughly chopped
1/2 medium onion, roughly chopped
1 bay leaf
Kosher salt
2 tsp dried Italian herb blend
Freshly ground black pepper
1/2 oz. dried porcini mushrooms, crumbled if large, optional
One 14-ounce can whole tomatoes, with juice
3 cups cleaned baby spinach leaves (about 3 ounces)
1/4 cup freshly grated Parmesan Balsamic vinegar, for drizzling
Extra-virgin olive oil, for drizzling

PROCEDURE

1) Combine the beans, carrots, barley, garlic, onions, celery, bay leaf, 1 1/2 tablespoons of salt, herbs, and mushrooms in the Instant Pot.
2) Add 6 cups of water.
3) Add the tomatoes.
4) Cook on low for 8 hours.
5) Add the cheese and spinach, and let it sit for around 5 minutes, or until the spinach wilts.
6) Season with pepper and salt.

7) Serve the soup hot and garnished with olive oil and vinegar.

Nutrition Facts: Serving size: 1/8 of a recipe (5.6 ounces). Calories: 124.9, Total Fat: 0.52 g, Cholesterol: 0 mg, Sodium: 179.88 mg, Potassium: 484.15 mg,   Total Carbohydrates: 26.42 g, Protein: 5.03 g

CHICKEN TORTILLA SOUP

SERVINGS: 4

This delicious Spanish inspired soup is simple and easy to prepare using the slow cooker feature of the Instant Pot.

INGREDIENTS

FOR SOUP:

1 Tbsp. olive oil
1 medium onion, chopped
2 cloves garlic, minced
2 6-inch corn tortillas, chopped into 1-inch squares
2 Tbsp. fresh cilantro, chopped
1 very large ripe tomato, chopped
1 15 oz. can black beans (or equivalent amount cooked beans)
1 cup frozen corn
3-4 cups chicken broth (or 3-4 cups water + 1 tbsp. 'Better Than Bouillon')
2 tsp chili powder
1 tsp ground cumin
1/4 tsp ground cayenne pepper
1 bay leaf
3 chicken breasts (roughly 12-16 oz.)

TO SERVE:

Corn tortillas, sliced into strips
Canola (or other) oil for frying
Fresh cilantro
Grated cheese
Fresh lime juice

PROCEDURE

1) In the Instant Pot, sauté the onion in the olive oil until the onion is soft.

2) Add the garlic, cilantro and tortilla squares. Cook for an additional

124

minute, stirring frequently.

3) Add the tomato, black beans, corn, spices, chicken breasts and 3 cups of broth. Cook for an additional minute.

4) Pressure cook on high for 4 minutes.

5) While the soup cooks, prepare the toppings.

6) Once the cooking is complete, remove the chicken breasts and shred the meat.

7) Return the chicken to the pot and mix well with the soup.

8) Serve the soup hot and garnished with cilantro, cheese, lime juice and the tortilla strips.

Nutrition Facts: Serving size: 1/4 of a recipe (19.1 ounces). Calories: 485.49, Total Fat: 14.15 g, Cholesterol: 61.06 mg, Sodium: 933.3 mg, Potassium: 1,093.38 mg,   Total Carbohydrates: 51.07 g, Protein: 40.37 g

CREAM OF BROCCOLI

SERVINGS: 6

This creamy soup is full of flavor but simple to make with the pressure function. Cooking on high pressure cuts down on cooking time while keeping the soup packed with nutrients.

INGREDIENTS

3 lbs. fresh broccoli
1 head of garlic
1 large onion
2 stalks of celery
1 cup of carrot (1/4" dice) (optional)
¼ tsp baking soda
1 Tbsp. Chicken Base or Vegetable Base
1 (15-ounce) can / 2 cups chicken or vegetable stock
2– 3 tablespoons olive oil
1 Tbsp. fresh lemon juice
Coarse kosher salt
Coarsely ground pepper
1 – 2 cups of milk / half and half / cream
1 fresh lemon
Sourdough or other rustic bread (optional)
Cheddar cheese (optional)

PROCEDURE

1) Wash the broccoli and trim, removing the florets. Cut the florets close to the head.
2) Dice the onions, celery and carrots.
3) In the Instant Pot, combine the vegetables, 1 cup of broth, and 1 tablespoon of base and ¼ teaspoon of baking soda.
4) Cook on high pressure for 20 minutes.
5) Puree the vegetables with a blender or food processor until completely smooth.

6) Add the cream and thoroughly combine.
7) Add the lemon juice and salt and pepper to taste.
8) Serve hot.

Nutrition Facts: Serving size: 1/6 of a recipe (17 ounces). Calories: 259.1, Total Fat: 11.2 g, Cholesterol: 3.08 mg, Sodium: 723.95 mg, Potassium: 1,063.51 mg, Total Carbohydrates: 30.06 g, Protein: 14.48 g

---

FRENCH ONION SOUP

SERVINGS: 4

This traditional soup is rich and full for flavor. It's simple and delicious. It'll quickly become a favorite recipe.

INGREDIENTS

4 medium onions, peeled and sliced
1 quart beef stock
2 sprigs of fresh thyme
½ cupsherry
8 slices Swiss cheese
6 slices Italian bread, toasted
1 tsp sea salt
1 tsp freshly ground black pepper
1 bay leaf
3 Tbsp. butter

PROCEDURE

1) Melt the butter using the sauté option. Caramelize the onions in the butter until they are golden brown.
2) Add the thyme, salt, pepper and sherry. Cook on low pressure for 15 minutes.
3) Allow the pressure to slowly release.
4) Add the beef stock and cook on low pressure for 12 minutes. Slowly release the pressure.
5) Add the bread on top of the onions and then a layer of cheese.
6) Close the lid and allow the cheese to melt.
7) Open the release and serve the soup hot.

Nutrition Facts: Serving size: 1/4 of a recipe (18.1 ounces). Calories: 537.42, Total Fat: 26.86 g, Cholesterol: 74.42 mg, Sodium: 6,739.45 mg, Potassium: 442.35 mg,   Total Carbohydrates: 42.6 g, Protein: 23.77 g

---

FRESH LEMON & GARLIC LAMB STEW

SERVINGS: 8

This stew brings the delicious flavors of the Mediterranean together into a scrumptious stew. Your mouth will be watering from the scent alone, and just wait until you taste the tender lamb infused with the rich garlic and citrusy lemon.

INGREDIENTS

2 Tbsp. olive oil
3 lb. lamb stew meat, cut into 2-inch pieces
Salt & Pepper to taste
3 cloves garlic, minced
6 Tbsp. freshly squeezed lemon juice
6 Tbsp. chicken stock

PROCEDURE

1) Using the sauté function, brown the meat in the oil until golden.
2) Add the remaining ingredients and then cook on high pressure for 15 minutes.
3) Rapidly release the remaining pressure.
4) Serve over noodles and garnished with grated cheese.

Nutrition Facts: Serving size: 1/8 of a recipe (4.6 ounces). Calories: 263.29, Total Fat: 12.45 g, Cholesterol: 110.16 mg, Sodium: 141.45 mg, Potassium: 291.2 mg,   Total Carbohydrates: 1.2 g, Protein: 34.7 g

---

GARLIC & CHICKEN STEW

SERVINGS: 6

This stew has all the familiar flavors of fall. This is perfect for a cool day.

INGREDIENTS

2 lbs. chicken breasts
2 Tbsp. oil
5 cloves garlic, chopped
1 russet potato, halved and thinly sliced
1 sweet potato, halved and thinly sliced
½ cupdried lentils
½ cup long-grain brown rice
1 Tbsp. kosher salt
1 tsp cayenne (optional)
½ tsp ground ginger
½ tsp ground coriander
2 cups chicken broth
2 cups water

PROCEDURE

1) Using the sauté function, brown the chicken on all sides.
2) Add the garlic, potatoes, lentils, rice, and seasonings. Mix well.
3) Add the broth and water. Make sure all the chicken has been covered with liquid.
4) Cook on high pressure for 10 minutes. Release using the quick release button.
5) Serve immediately.

Nutrition Facts: Serving size: 1/6 of a recipe (15 ounces). Calories: 410.33, Total Fat: 9.71 g, Cholesterol: 96.77 mg, Sodium: 1,383.09 mg, Potassium: 1,147.63 mg,   Total Carbohydrates: 39.4 g, Protein: 40.71 g

---

HEARTY BEEF STEW

SERVINGS: 6

This flavorful stew has incredibly tender beef. It's perfect for a winter Sunday dinner.

INGREDIENTS

4 Tbsp. flour
2 Tbsp. olive oil
1 ½ lbs. beef roast, cut into cubes
1 large onion, chopped
3 cloves garlic, minced
2 cups beef stock
1 cup water
1 bay leaf
½ tsp dried thyme
3 – 4 medium potatoes, cut into cubes
2 carrots, peeled and sliced
2 celery stocks, sliced
Salt & Pepper to taste

PROCEDURE

1) Dredge the beef chunks in the flour and then brown in the oil on the sauté function.
2) Add the garlic and onion, sauté for 2 minutes.
3) Add half of the beef broth and stir to deglaze the pan.
4) Add the seasonings. Cook on low pressure for 12 minutes.
5) Use the quick release button and then add the remaining ingredients.
6) Cook on high pressure for 4 – 5 minutes.
7) Allow the pressure to slowly release.
8) Serve hot, with a side of crackers or homemade rolls.

Nutrition Facts: Serving size: 1/6 of a recipe (14.1 ounces). Calories: 492.79, Total Fat: 32.34 g, Cholesterol: 79.38 mg, Sodium: 447.88 mg, Potassium: 926.35 mg,   Total Carbohydrates: 25.59 g, Protein: 24.12 g

---

NEW ENGLAND CLAM CHOWDER

SERVINGS: 6

This clam chowder is traditional of the Northeastern US. It's rich and creamy flavor is the perfect comfort food.

INGREDIENTS

25 little neck clams
6 cups clam broth
3 Tbsp. butter
3 Tbsp. flour
½ lb. bacon, diced
1 medium onion, sliced
3 stalks celery, diced
½ red pepper, diced
2 large potatoes, diced
2 bay leaves
1 sprig thyme
Sea salt & fresh ground black pepper
¾ cups heavy cream

PROCEDURE

1) Cook the bacon on the sauté function until it's crispy.
2) Add the vegetables and butter, cooking for 10 minutes.
3) Add the flour and mix well to coat all the vegetables and bacon. Continue to cook for another 2 minutes.
4) Add the remaining ingredients – except the cream- and blend the mixture well.
5) Cook on high pressure for 1 minutes, then rapidly release the remaining pressure.
6) Add the cream and mix well.

7) Serve hot.

Nutrition Facts: Serving size: 1/6 of a recipe (17.1 ounces). Calories: 561.07, Total Fat: 32.29 g, Cholesterol: 81.05 mg, Sodium: 2,321.82 mg, Potassium: 880.86 mg, Total Carbohydrates: 46.31 g, Protein: 21.57 g

---

ONION CHICKEN SOUP

SERVINGS: 6

This delicious soup is simple and easy to make. Add color, nutrients and flavor by adding your choice of vegetables.

INGREDIENTS

1 1/2 lbs. boneless skinless chicken, cut into pieces
1 pkg (1.2 oz.) onion soup mix
2 cups water
1 cup vegetables of choice (carrots, broccoli, green beans, summer squash, peas, etc)

PROCEDURE

1) Layer the chicken and vegetables in the pot.
2) Add the water and soup mix.
3) Cook on low pressure for 15 minutes.
4) Allow the pressure to decrease. Serve hot.

Nutrition Facts: Serving size: 1/6 of a recipe (14.6 ounces). Calories: 108.01, Total Fat: 1.86 g, Cholesterol: 0 mg, Sodium: 1,335.95 mg, Potassium: 426.03 mg, Total Carbohydrates: 15.37 g, Protein: 8.13 g

QUICK & EASY CHILI

SERVINGS: 6

This traditional chili is quick to make with the Instant Pot. It's perfect for a cool day. Serve with rice, sour cream, cheese and cornbread. This chili is also a great topping for a baked potato bar.

INGREDIENTS

1 ½ lbs. ground beef
1 lbs. mixed dried beans, soaked overnight
1 ¾ lbs. canned, diced tomatoes
17 oz. beef stock
1 large onion, chopped
6 cloves garlic, minced
1 Tbsp. oil
3 Tbsp. chili powder
Salt & Pepper to taste

PROCEDURE

1) Brown the ground beef on the sauté setting with the oil.
2) Once the beef is browned, add the onions and garlic. Sauté for 2 minutes.
3) Add the remaining ingredients and stir to combine.
4) Cook on low pressure for 25 minutes.
5) Allow the pressure to slowly release.
6) Season to taste, if more seasonings are desired.
7) Serve hot and topped with favorite toppings.

Nutrition Facts: Serving size: 1/6 of a recipe (18.4 ounces). Calories: 565.68, Total Fat: 27.43 g, Cholesterol: 85.05 mg, Sodium: 1,202.94 mg, Potassium: 1,188.78 mg, Total Carbohydrates: 45.47 g, Protein: 35.37 g

---

PORK & HOMINY STEW

SERVINGS: 2

This delicious stew is easy and quick to make on the high pressure setting. It has a hint of spiciness, but is delicious and full of flavor and nutrients.

INGREDIENTS

> 1 ¼ lbs. pork shoulder, cubed into bite-size pieces
> Salt
> 2 Tbsp. olive oil
> ½ cup roughly chopped yellow onion
> 4 garlic cloves, roughly chopped
> 1 tsp pureed chipotle in adobo sauce
> ¼ tspcumin
> ½ tsp oregano
> 3 ¼ cups (2 cans) low-sodium chicken broth, divided
> 1 (29 ounce) can hominy, drained and rinsed
> 1 (14.5 ounce) can diced tomatoes
> Chopped cilantro
> Sliced jalapeños

PROCEDURE

1) Season the pork with salt and pepper.
2) Place the pork in the Instant Pot with the oil. Brown the pork on all sides.
3) Add the onion, garlic, chipotle, cumin, oregano and chicken broth.
4) Cook on medium pressure for 13 minutes.
5) Add the remaining broth, hominy and tomatoes with their juice.

6) Bring the pot back to a simmer. Cook until the hominy is tender, about 15 – 20 minutes.

Nutrition Facts: Serving size: 1/2 of a recipe (45.2 ounces). Calories: 994.03, Total Fat: 54 g, Cholesterol: 175.77 mg, Sodium: 1,372.93 mg, Potassium: 1,883.4 mg, Total Carbohydrates: 63.56 g, Protein: 64.66 g

---

PUMPKIN SOUP WITH CHICKEN & ORZO

SERVINGS: 4

Have dinner ready in minutes with this fall inspired soup.

INGREDIENTS

2 cups of fresh pumpkin or butternut squash (peeled, and cubed)
3 Tbsp. butter
½ cup onions, diced
½ cup celery, diced
½ cup carrots, diced
1 garlic clove, minced
3 cups chicken stock
1 can (14 oz.) diced tomatoes with juice
½ tspItalian seasoning
1/8 tsp dried red pepper flakes
¼ tsp freshly ground black pepper
1/8 tsp freshly grated nutmeg
1 cup orzo, cooked
1 cup chicken, cooked and diced
1 to 1 ½ cup half and half
Green onion tops, sliced very thin (save for garnish)

PROCEDURE

1) Sauté the onions, celery and carrots in the butter until the onions are translucent, about 5 minutes.
2) Add the garlic and cook for an additional minute.
3) Add the chicken stock, tomatoes and squash.
4) Season with the red pepper flakes, pepper and nutmeg. Stir until thoroughly combined.
5) Cook on high pressure for 10 minutes.
6) Puree the mixture using an immersion blender or remove the mixture from the pot and use a blender or food processor. Once pureed, return the mixture to the pot.

7) Add the chicken, orzo and cream. Simmer until the chicken is heated though.
8) Season to taste with salt and pepper.
9) Serve hot, garnished with the green onions and a dollop of cream.

Nutrition Facts: Serving size: 1/4 of a recipe (17.7 ounces). Calories: 393.28, Total Fat: 17, Cholesterol: 45.28 mg, Sodium: 1,1001.15 mg, Potassium: 722.1 mg, Total Carbohydrates: 45.24 g, Protein: 13.41 g

SEAFOOD CHOWDER

SERVINGS: 6

This rich and creamy chowder will bring back memories of beaches and boat rides on the ocean.

INGREDIENTS

1 sweet onion, diced
3 – 5 cloves garlic, minced
½ red bell pepper, finely diced
1 stalk celery, finely diced
2 red potatoes, finely diced
13 oz. clams, minced and juices reserved
6 oz. canned or imitation crab
1 – 2 white fish fillet, cut into chunks
Salt & Pepper to taste
4 sprigs thyme
3 bay leaves
3 ½ cups liquid (reserved juices and water)
2 cups cream or half and half

PROCEDURE

1) Combine all the ingredients, except the cream, in the Instant Pot.
2) Cook on high for 5 minutes.
3) Slowly release the pressure and stir in the cream.
4) Season to taste and bring back to simmer using the sauté function.
5) Serve hot with oyster crackers.

Nutrition Facts: Serving size: 1/6 of a recipe (14.8 ounces). Calories: 301.89, Total Fat: 15.82 g, Cholesterol: 93.8 mg, Sodium: 679.68 mg, Potassium: 580.08 mg, Total Carbohydrates: 20.38 g, Protein: 19.7 g

---

VEAL SHANK BARLEY SOUP

SERVINGS: 8

This soup is simple and delicious. If you don't have veal, just use a beef roast. It's perfect for a busy night when you want comfort food.

INGREDIENTS

2 Tbsp. olive oil
3 lbs. veal shank, cut into 3 equal portions
1 large onion, finely chopped
5 sticks celery, finely chopped
6 carrots, peeled and finely chopped
3 potatoes, peeled and cubed
6 cups chicken, beef or vegetable stock
1 ¼ cup pearl barley

PROCEDURE

1) Sear the veal shanks on the sauté setting with 1 Tbsp. of oil.
2) Once they have been browned on all sides, remove from the pot.
3) Add the remaining with the onion and celery. Sauté until the onion is translucent, about 5 – 6 minutes.
4) Add the remaining ingredients and cook on low pressure for 20 – 30 minutes, or until the veal is tender.
5) Allow the pressure to slowly reduce.
6) Remove the meat from the bones and shred the meat. Return the meat to the soup.
7) Serve hot.

Nutrition Facts: Serving size: 1/8 of a recipe (18.9 ounces). Calories: 449.26, Total Fat: 10.21 g, Cholesterol: 132.68 mg, Sodium: 728.81 mg, Potassium: 1,472.26 mg, Total Carbohydrates: 43.92 g, Protein: 44.47 g

---

VIETNAMESE SEAFOOD STEW

SERVINGS: 6

This seafood stew brings the delicious flavor of Vietnam. It's rich and savory, with the cumin, saffron and curry adding the distinct flavors of the jungle.

INGREDIENTS

> *2 cloves garlic, minced*
> *1 small apple, peeled and diced*
> *1 banana, peeled and sliced*
> *½ cupraisins*
> *2 Tbsp. light brown sugar*
> *¼ tsp ground cumin*
> *¼ tsp saffron*
> *2 Tbsp. curry powder*
> *2 cups chicken broth*
> *2 cups unsweetened coconut milk*
> *2 Tbsp. lemon or lime juice*
> *1 tsp Worcestershire sauce*
> *¾ cupheavy cream*
> *32 shrimp, peeled and deveined*
> *16 sea scallops*
> *1 lb. firm white fish (halibut, cod or snapper)*
> *1 small red bell pepper, diced*
> *½ cupcooked chickpeas*
> *¼ cupfresh cilantro, minced*

PROCEDURE

1) In the pressure cooker, combine the garlic, apple, raisins, banana, brown sugar, cumin, saffron, curry powder, broth, coconut milk, lemon or lime juice and Worcestershire sauce. Mix to combine well and then cook on low pressure for 10 minutes.
2) While the mixture is cooking, cut the fish into bite sized cubes.

142

3) Use the quick release button to reduce the pressure.
4) Puree the mixture in a blender, food processor or using an immersion blender.
5) Add the cream and season to taste.
6) Add the shrimp, scallops, fish, bell peppers and chickpeas.
7) Cook on high pressure for 1 minute, then use the rapid release to get rid of the pressure.
8) Serve over rice and garnish with cilantro.

Nutrition Facts: Serving size: 1/6 of a recipe (15.7 ounces). Calories: 502.66, Total Fat: 29.32 g, Cholesterol: 121.14 mg, Sodium: 716.51 mg, Potassium: 1,018 mg, Total Carbohydrates: 36.13 g, Protein: 27.88 g

---

VEAL STEW

SERVINGS: 6

This stew is full of flavor with a distinct Mediterranean flavor.

INGREDIENTS

1 ½ lbs. lean veal stew meat
½ cupflour
3 Tbsp. oil
1 onion, diced
4 cloves garlic, minced
1 can (15 oz.) diced tomatoes
½ cupwhite wine
1 cup chicken broth
¼ tsp ground thyme
½ tsp salt
¼ tsp pepper
1 bay leaf

PROCEDURE

1) Cut the veal into 1-inch chunks and then dredge the chunks in flour.
2) Brown the veal in the oil on the sauté setting.
3) Add the onions and garlic and sauté for 2 minutes, or until the onions are translucent.
4) Add the remaining ingredients to the Instant Pot. Cook on high pressure for 15 minutes.
5) Allow the pressure to slowly release.
6) Serve with a side of rice, if desired.

Nutrition Facts: Serving size: 1/6 of a recipe (10.2 ounces). Calories: 277.22, Total Fat: 10.71 g, Cholesterol: 88.45 mg, Sodium: 498.28 mg, Potassium: 657.44 mg, Total Carbohydrates: 14.31 g, Protein: 26.65 g

---

6

DESSERTS

APPLE CINNAMON FLAN

SERVINGS: 4

This flan is elegant and delicious. It can make a perfect end to an elegant meal.

INGREDIENTS

5 Tbsp. maple syrup
¼ tsp cinnamon
2 apples, peeled and thinly sliced
3 whole eggs
3 egg yolks
¼ tsp vanilla
6 Tbsp. sugar
2 ½ cups milk

PROCEDURE

1) Grease 4 – 6 ramekins (as many as will fit into your cooker).
2) In a small pan, combine the maple syrup and cinnamon.
3) Add the sliced apples and cook for 4 minutes.
4) Meanwhile, in a separate bowl, whisk together the eggs and egg yolks.
5) Add the vanilla, sugar and milk.
6) Once the apples are tender, evenly divide them into the bottom of the ramekins.
7) Gently pour an equal amount of the egg mixture into each ramekin.
8) Wrap the ramekins with foil and place in the cooker on top of a trivet.
9) Add enough water to the cooker so the water comes within 1-inch of the top of the ramekins.
10) Cook on high pressure for 6 minutes.
11) Allow the pressure to slowly release.
12) Remove the ramekins from the cooker and refrigerate for 2 hours.

13) Use a knife to gently release the edge of the custard from the ramekin and turn upside down on a plate to serve.

Nutrition Facts: Serving size: 1/4 of a recipe (11.1 ounces). Calories: 345.14, Total Fat: 10.02 g, Cholesterol: 286.78 mg, Sodium: 134.82 mg, Potassium: 407.12 mg,   Total Carbohydrates: 53.39 g, Protein: 11.91 g

---

APPLE CRUMB CAKE

SERVINGS: 6

This is a simple dessert that's perfect for fall. It's easy to make a gluten free version – simply use a gluten free flour such as rice flour.

INGREDIENTS

> 6 small red apples
> 6 Tbsp. melted butter
> 2/3 cup granulated sugar
> 1 2/3 cup old fashioned oats
> 2 Tbsp. flour
> 1 tsp ground ginger
> 1 tsp ground cinnamon
> 1 Tbsp. lemon juice

PROCEDURE

1) In a small bowl, combine the sugar, oats, ginger, cinnamon, butter and lemon juice.
2) Peel and thinly slice the apples.
3) Grease a small bowl or pan (one that will fit into the cooker) with butter. Place the apples into the pan.
4) Toss the apples with the flour to coat the apples.
5) Add the topping on top of the apples.
6) Place a trivet in the bottom of the cooker and add 1 ½ cups of water to the cooker.
7) Place the baking dish with the apples on top of the trivet.
8) Cook on low pressure for 10 minutes.
9) Allow the pressure to slowly release.
10) Serve warm with whipped cream or ice cream.

Nutrition Facts: Serving size: 1/6 of a recipe (12.9 ounces). Calories: 600.15, Total Fat: 14.74 g, Cholesterol: 30.53 mg, Sodium: 56.02 mg, Potassium: 472.81 mg,   Total Carbohydrates: 111.56 g, Protein: 8.3 g

---

CREAMY RICE PUDDING

SERVINGS: 6

Use the Instant Pot to create a delicious and creamy rice pudding in no time! The rice function ensures that you have moist and tender rice every time. This classic rice pudding is a perfect dessert.

INGREDIENTS

1 ½ cups Arborio Rice
¾ cups sugar
½ tspsalt
5 cups milk (1% or 2%)
2 eggs
1 cup half and half
1 ½ tsp vanilla extract
1 cup golden raisins
Cinnamon if desired

PROCEDURE

1) Combine the rice, sugar, salt and milk in the Instant Pot.
2) Bring the mixture to a boil using the Sauté feature. Stir frequently and continue cooking until the sugar completely dissolves.
3) Once the sugar dissolves and the mixture comes to a boil, cover the mixture and start the rice function.
4) Meanwhile, whisk together the eggs, half and half and vanilla extract.
5) Once the rice is finished cooking, wait for 15 minutes before using the quick pressure release.
6) Gently stir the egg mixture into the rice. Add raisins, if using.
7) Sauté the mixture, uncovered, until it begins to boil.
8) Serve the rice pudding immediately or refrigerate immediately.

Nutrition Facts: Serving size: 1/6 of a recipe (12.8 ounces). Calories: 530.26, Total Fat: 10.38 g, Cholesterol: 93.19 mg, Sodium: 341.67 mg, Potassium: 569.21 mg,   Total Carbohydrates: 96 g, Protein: 14.32 g

BLUEBERRY PUDDING

SERVINGS: 4

This is a summery and tasty pudding. It's simple to make, but be sure to plan ahead so it has time to cool.

INGREDIENTS

> 1 cup flour
> 1 ½ tsp baking powder
> ½ tsp salt
> ½ cup butter, cut into small pieces
> ½ cupgranulated sugar
> 1 egg, beaten
> 5 oz. milk
> ½ lb. blueberries, fresh or frozen

PROCEDURE

1) In a large bowl, combine the flour, baking powder and salt.
2) Cut the butter into the mixture until it resembles coarse crumbs.
3) Add the egg and milk, stir until just combined.
4) Fold in the blueberries.
5) Grease a bowl or dish that fits into the cooker.
6) Pour the blueberry mixture into the bowl and cover with parchment paper. Tie the parchment paper around the edge of the bowl.
7) Place a trivet in the bottom of the cooker and place the bowl on top of the trivet.
8) Add water to the cooker, but be sure it doesn't come more than ½ inch from the top of the bowl.
9) Cook on low pressure for 25 – 30 minutes.
10) Use the rapid release button to quickly release the pressure.
11) Remove the bowl from the cooker.
12) Use a knife to gently loosen the edge of the pudding.

13) Serve with whipped cream, if desired.

Nutrition Facts: Serving size: 1/4 of a recipe (6.8 ounces). Calories: 482.78, Total Fat: 25.4 g, Cholesterol: 110.34 mg, Sodium: 512.5 mg, Potassium: 151.67 mg, Total Carbohydrates: 59.34 g, Protein: 6.63 g

CHOCOLATE CHIP CHEESECAKE

SERVINGS: 12

This delicious cheesecake doesn't just have chocolate chips, the traditional cheesecake crust has been replaced by a moist chocolate brownie. Cooking this in the pressure cooker makes the cheesecake quick and easy to make as well as moist. It makes a perfect end to any meal.

INGREDIENTS

BROWNIE BOTTOM INGREDIENTS:

½ cupbutter
¼ cupCocoa Powder
½ cupsugar
¾ cupwhite flour
¾ tsp baking powder
¼ tsp salt
1 Tbsp. Honey
2 eggs
2 cups water

CHEESECAKE FILLING INGREDIENTS:

3 (8 ounce) packages of cream cheese softened and at room temperature
1 (14 oz.) can of Eagle Brand Sweetened Condensed Milk
3 large eggs
2 tsp vanilla extract
½ cupchocolate chips
Topping Ingredients:
1 cup cream heated to boiling
9 oz. chocolate chips
Whipping cream and strawberries optional

PROCEDURE

FOR THE CRUST:

1) Melt the butter and mix in the cocoa powder. Set aside to cool.
2) Meanwhile, in a large bowl, whisk together the sugar, flour, baking powder and salt.
3) Whisk in the honey, eggs, and cocoa mixture.
4) Lightly grease an 8 inch spring form pan. Gently pour the brownie mixture into the bottom of the pan.
5) Pour 2 cups of water into the Instant Pot and then place a trivet or steamer tray into the water.
6) Cook the brownie mixture on high pressure for 35 minutes.
7) While the brownie is cooking, prepare the filling.

FOR THE FILLING:

1) Beat the cream cheese until fluffy and smooth.
2) Gradually beat in the sweetened condensed milk and beat until combined.
3) Add the eggs and vanilla to the mixture and beat just combined.
4) Fold in the chocolate chips.
5) Once the brownie finishes, remove the crust from the Instant Pot and gently pour the filling over the crust.
6) Return the pan to the Instant Pot and cook on high for 15 minutes.
7) Once the cooker is done, turn it to "Keep Warm" and leave for 6 hours.
8) Remove from the cooker and let it cool.

FOR THE FILLING:

1) Heat 8 ounces of cream cheese to a simmer.
2) Add 9 ounces of chocolate chips and stir the mixture until the chocolate chips have melted and been thoroughly mixed in.
3) Serve the cheesecake with the chocolate sauce drizzled on top.

Nutrition Facts: Serving size: 1/12 of a recipe (8.5 ounces). Calories:710.64, Total Fat: 49.08 g, Cholesterol: 202.73 mg, Sodium: 360.73 mg, Potassium: 327.72 mg, Total Carbohydrates: 62.12 g, Protein: 12.34 g

FUDGE

SERVINGS: 12

This delicious sweet treat isn't just for holidays. It's perfect for office parties, potlucks, get togethers or to satisfy a sweet tooth.

INGREDIENTS

1 can (14 oz.) sweetened condensed milk
2 (6 oz. each) pkg semi-sweet chocolate chips
1 cup chopped walnuts
1 tsp vanilla
2 cups water

PROCEDURE

1) In a small steel bowl, combine the milk and chocolate chips.
2) Place a trivet on the bottom of the cooker and add the water.
3) Cover the bowl with foil and place on the trivet.
4) Cook on high pressure for 5 minutes.
5) Release the pressure quickly.
6) Remove the bowl from the cooker and add the nuts and vanilla. Stir until well combined.
7) Remove from the bowl and smooth into a baking dish lined with aluminum foil. Make sure to leave enough foil over the top of the pan so that there are "handles", making removal easy.
8) Chill.
9) Remove the fudge by using the "handles" to pull the foil out of the pan. Peel the foil off the fudge and cut the fudge before serving.

Nutrition Facts: Serving size: 1/12 of a recipe (3.6 ounces). Calories: 280.82, Total Fat: 17.04 g, Cholesterol: 8.5 mg, Sodium: 36.28 mg, Potassium: 136.66 mg, Total Carbohydrates: 32.95 g, Protein: 4.65 g

---

LEMON CRÈME

SERVINGS: 4

This crème is rich and delicious, but not overwhelming. It's a perfect end to any meal. Top with fresh fruit like blackberries, blueberries or raspberries with a mint leaf to make it look elegant.

INGREDIENTS

1 cup whole milk
1 cup cream
6 egg yolks
Zest from 1 lemon
2/3 cup white sugar

PROCEDURE

1) Combine the milk, cream and lemon zest in a small sauce pan. Bring to a boil, then shut off the heat and allow it to cool.
2) Meanwhile, add a trivet to the bottom of the cooker and add 1 cup of water.
3) In a bowl, combine the egg yolks and sugar. Whisk together until the sugar is completely dissolved.
4) Combine the egg mixture with the cream mixture. Do not whip the mixture, but mix until just combined.
5) Evenly divide the mixture into 4 ramekins and then place the ramekins in the steamer basket.
6) Place the basket on the trivet and cook on high pressure for 10 minutes.
7) Allow the cooker to slowly cool and then remove the custards.
8) Allow the custards to cool for 30 – 45 minutes.
9) Once cooled, garnish and serve.

Nutrition Facts: Serving size: 1/4 of a recipe (6.4 ounces). Calories: 452.37, Total Fat: 30.61 g, Cholesterol: 357.78, Sodium: 61.22 mg, Potassium: 155.35 mg,   Total Carbohydrates: 39.05 g, Protein: 7.11 g

---

MEYER LEMON CHEESECAKE

SERVINGS: 8

Meyer lemons are smaller, sweeter and less acidic than regular lemons. This delicious cheesecake has a sweet and savory lemon flavor that will leave you delighted.

INGREDIENTS

CRUST

8 oz. shortbread cookies (about 10 large shortbread cookies)
2 Tbsp. butter, melted

FILLING

2 - 8 oz. packages cream cheese, at room temperature
1/2 cup granulated sugar
1/4 cup sour cream
1 Tbsp. Meyer lemon juice
2 tsp grated lemon zest
1/2 tsp vanilla extract
2 large eggs

PROCEDURE

1) Crush the cookies into crumbs. Combine the crumbs with the butter and mix well.
2) Press into the bottom of a 7" spring form pan.
3) Freeze the pan until ready to use.
4) In a large bowl, combine the cream cheese and sugar until smooth and fluffy. Add the sour cream, lemon juice, lemon zest and vanilla. Blend until all ingredients are well combined.
5) Beat the eggs into the mixture, one at a time. Beat until each egg is combined, do not overbeat.
6) Pour the batter into the pan on top of the crumbs.
7) In the bottom of the Instant Pot, pour 2 cups of water and place a trivet.

8) Place the pan on the trivet and cook on high pressure for 10 minutes.
9) Allow the pressure to decrease for 10 minutes, and then use the quick release.
10) Remove the pan from the cooker and place on a wire rack to cool.
11) Once the cheesecake is completely cooled, refrigerate, covered, for at least 4 hours, or overnight.

Nutrition Facts: Serving size: 1/8 of a recipe (4.4 ounces). Calories: 427.06, Total Fat: 31.23 g, Cholesterol: 120.24 mg, Sodium: 261.66 mg, Potassium: 126.61 mg,   Total Carbohydrates: 34.04 g, Protein: 6.45 g

PUMPKIN CHOCOLATE CHIP BUNDT CAKE

SERVINGS: 8

This delicious Bundt cake is moist and easy to make. It's the perfect fall dessert, but don't wait for fall to try it.

INGREDIENTS

1 1/2 cups all-purpose flour
1/2 tsp pumpkin pie spice
1 tsp ground cinnamon
1/4 tsp salt
1/2 tsp baking soda
1/2 tsp baking powder
1/2 cup (1 stick) butter, soften
1 cup granulated sugar
2 large eggs
1 cup pumpkin puree
3/4 cup mini chocolate chips

PROCEDURE

1) Mix together the flour, salt, spices, baking powder and baking soda.
2) In a mixer, cream the butter and sugar until they are fluffy.
3) Add in the eggs to the butter one at a time and mix well after adding each egg.
4) Add the pumpkin and mix until well combined.
5) Slowly add the dry ingredients to the pumpkin mixture until the dry ingredients are combined.
6) Fold in the chocolate chips.
7) Lightly grease a half sized Bundt pan and pour the batter into it.
8) Cover the pan with foil.
9) Add 1 ½ cups of water to the cooker and place a trivet or steamer tray in the bottom.
10) Place the pan on top of the trivet and cook on high pressure for 25 minutes.

11) Allow the pressure to decrease for 10 minutes, then use the quick release.
12) Remove the pan and allow it to cool, uncovered, for 10 minutes.
13) Remove the cake from the pan and cool it the rest of the way on a wire rack

Nutrition Facts: Serving size: 1/8 of a recipe (4.3 ounces). Calories: 388.84, Total Fat: 17.75 g, Cholesterol: 77 mg, Sodium: 277.46 mg, Potassium: 111.5 mg,   Total Carbohydrates: 55.86g, Protein: 5.13 g

QUICK AND EASY HAZELNUT FLAN

SERVINGS: 8

This delicious hazelnut flan is tender and moist. It's simple and quick to make. It'll quickly become a favorite dessert.

INGREDIENTS

FOR THE CARAMEL:

> 3/4 cup granulated sugar
> 1/4 cup water

FOR THE CUSTARD:

> 3 whole eggs
> 2 egg yolks
> 1/3 cup granulated sugar
> Pinch of salt
> 2 cups whole milk
> 1/2 cup whipping cream
> 1 tsp vanilla extract
> 2 Tbsp. Hazelnut syrup

PROCEDURE

PREPARE THE CARAMEL SAUCE:

1) Combine the sugar and water in a saucepan and bring the mixture to a boil. Boil for 2 minutes, covered. Remove the lid and continue cooking, without stirring, until the mixture is amber. Even though you should not stir the mixture, make sure to swirl the pan so that it doesn't burn.
2) Evenly divide the caramel sauce into 8 ungreased ramekins. Make sure the sauce completely coats the bottom of each ramekin.
3) Set the ramekins aside while the custard is prepared.

PREPARE THE CUSTARD:

1) In a medium saucepan, heat the milk to a simmer.
2) Meanwhile, whisk together the eggs and yolks with the sugar and salt.
3) Gradually add the hot milk to the eggs, whisking continually.
4) Whisk the cream and syrups into the egg mixture.
5) Strain the egg mixture into a large measuring cup.
6) Evenly divide the egg mixture into the 8 ramekins with the caramel sauce. Cover the ramekins with foil.
7) In the bottom of the Instant Pot, add 1 1/2 cups of water. Place a trivet in the middle.
8) Place the ramekins on top of the trivet, making a second layer divided by another trivet if necessary.
9) Cook on high pressure for 6 minutes.
10) Remove from the cooker and cool completely.
11) Refrigerate for 4 hours or overnight.
12) Before serving, separate the custard from the ramekin by running a thin knife around the edge.
13) Turn the custard out onto a plate so the caramel sauce is on the top.
14) Serve garnished with whipped cream and chopped hazelnuts, if desired.

Nutrition Facts: Serving size: 1/8 of a recipe (4.9 ounces). Calories: 249.33, Total Fat: 10.37 g, Cholesterol: 14.26 mg, Sodium: 105.13 mg, Potassium: 125.67 mg, Total Carbohydrates: 347.65 g, Protein: 5.24 g

---

STEAMED BREAD PUDDING

SERVINGS: 6

This is one of the tastiest and quickest bread puddings you will ever make. The instant pot allows the bread pudding to cook quickly and stay moist and tender. This bread pudding is delicious when topped with caramel sauce and whipped cream.

INGREDIENTS

1 tsp coconut oil
1 cup Goya Coconut milk
1 cup whole milk
3 eggs, beaten
4 cup cubed stale bread
½ cupdried cranberries
1 tsp cinnamon
¼ tsp salt
½ tsp vanilla
Optional ingredients can be:
Coconut flakes
Macadamia nuts or other nuts such as walnuts or pecans Apple ½ of a fresh apple minced

PROCEDURE

1) Fill the Instant Pot with 2 cups of water and add the steam rack to the top.
2) Cut the bread into cubes.
3) Mix the remaining ingredients in a large bowl. Fold in the bread. Mix well.
4) Place the bread mixture in a casserole dish that will fit inside of the cooker.
5) Cover the casserole dish with wax paper and secure the paper with cooking twine or silicone bands that can withstand high temperatures.

6) Steam the bread mixture for 15 minutes.
7) Once the pressure has dropped, release the lid and remove the casserole dish. You may want to broil the bread pudding for 2 – 3 minutes to brown the top of the pudding.
8) Serve hot with caramel sauce.

Nutrition Facts: Serving size: 1/6 of a recipe (8.2 ounces). Calories: 594.62, Total Fat: 25.23 g, Cholesterol: 97.07 mg, Sodium: 551.12 mg, Potassium: 345.61 mg, Total Carbohydrates: 81.45 g, Protein: 13.27 g

PEARS IN RED WINE

SERVINGS: 6

This is a simple, elegant and delicious dessert

INGREDIENTS

6 green pears, peeled but with the stems intact
1 vanilla pod
1 clove
1 pinch of Cinnamon
¾ cupsugar
6 oz. red wine

PROCEDURE

1) Combine the wine, sugar, vanilla and cloves in the cooker. Turn the cooker on warm and stir in the sugar until it dissolves.
2) Add the pears, standing them up on their base. You may need to slice a piece of pear off the bottom to make sure it stands upright.
3) Cook on low pressure for 7 minutes.
4) Quickly release the pressure.
5) Serve hot and drizzle the wine sauce over the pears.

Nutrition Facts: Serving size: 1/6 of a recipe (2 ounces). Calories: 125.09, Total Fat: 0.07 g, Cholesterol: 0 mg, Sodium: 2.35 mg. Potassium: 43.06 mg,   Total Carbohydrates: 26.11 g, Protein: 0.04 g

---

TAPIOCA PUDDING

SERVINGS: 3

This is the easiest tapioca pudding that you'll ever make. It's easy and simple – no stirring or soaking!

INGREDIENTS

1/3 cup seed tapioca pearls
1 ¼ cup whole milk (or milk alternative)
½ cup water
½ cupsugar
½ lemon zested

PROCEDURE

1) Add 1 cup of water to the cooker.
2) In a heat proof bowl, combine the tapioca pearls, milk, water, zest and sugar. Mix until the sugar has dissolved.
3) Place the bowl in the cooker (you may want to make a foil "handle" to easily remove the bowl).
4) Cook on high for 8 minutes.
5) Allow the pressure to slowly release.
6) Once the pressure has released, let the tapioca sit for another 5 minutes.
7) Fluff the tapioca with a folk and then serve, garnished with fresh fruit, if desired.

Nutrition Facts: Serving size: 1/3 of a recipe (6.8 ounces). Calories: 251.89, Total Fat: 3.31 g, Cholesterol: 10.17 mg, Sodium: 45.46 mg, Potassium: 138.72 mg, Total Carbohydrates: 53.33 g, Protein: 3.25 g

---

Made in the USA
Lexington, KY
14 February 2016